WHEN WE ARE BOLD

Women Who Turn Our Upsidedown World Right

EDITED BY

RACHEL M. VINCENT

Art and Literature Mapalé & Publishing Inc.

Published by Art and Literature Mapalé & Publishing Inc.

Edited by Rachel M. Vincent
Foreword by Brené Brown
Cover design by Kimberly Glyder
Book design by Silvia Alfaro

Library and Archives Canada Cataloguing in Publication

When we are bold : women who turn our upsidedown world right / edited by Rachel M. Vincent.

ISBN 978-0-9949441-6-0 (paperback).--
ISBN 978-0-9949441-7-7 (hardback)

1. Women--Biography. 2. Women political activists--Biography. 3. Feminists--Biography. 4. Mothers--Biography. 5. Reconciliation. I. Vincent, Rachel M., editor

CT3202.W54 2016   920.72   C2016-905729-1

www.editorialmapale.com

EDITED BY

RACHEL M. VINCENT

WHEN
WE ARE
BOLD

Women Who Turn Our
Upsidedown World Right

Art and Literature Mapalé & Publishing Inc.

TABLE OF CONTENTS

FOREWORD

by Brené Brown

Courage is a heart word. The root of the word *courage* is *cor*—the Latin word for heart. In one of its earliest forms, the word *courage* meant "To speak one's mind by telling all one's heart." In today's media-saturated world, our definition of courage has shifted toward rating-generating displays of heroism, causing us to lose sight of what it means to be truly brave with our voice, our stories, and our truth. *When We Are Bold: Women Who Turn Our Upsidedown World Right* is not only a celebration of women peacemakers and the activists they've inspired, it is a call to courage. A call to all of us who have allowed activism to be defined as something that other people do, to those of us who have orphaned our voice and our story, and to every woman and man who has struggled or borne witness to injustices that left their hearts flooded with truth and stories that need to be spoken.

Much of the violence and unconscionable political rhetoric we see and hear today is about *power-over*—individuals and groups making a last stand, in part, to maintain or regain power over the bodies, minds, and future of women and girls. By definition, last stands are violent and fueled by fear, shame, and desperation. But as this collection of essays illuminates, our foremothers have forged an undeniable, hard-fought shift toward a vision of power that is shared, infinite, and just. As I read through these essays it was clear that their approaches to peacemaking and justice defy categorization. These women have taught us and continue to show us that there is not just one way to effectively claim and share power, but many ways to be true to who we are, how we show up, and what we believe while joining forces for change.

I had the great honor of teaching a course on global justice at the University of Houston Graduate College of Social Work with Nobel peace laureate Jody Williams. In my five years of co-teaching with Jody and in my ongoing work mentoring activists and organizers, I have learned that the greatest barrier to engagement is the belief that there is only one way to affect change and only one model of activism. Our task is not to rigidly define activism but to make room at the table for many methods, approaches, and voices. *When We Are Bold* shows us the power of that welcoming table.

In her essay on Nawal El Saadawi, Rana Husseini shares a quote from El Saadawi's novel, *Woman at Point Zero*, that beautifully captures the depth of courage inherent in truth-telling. In the novel, the authorities tell a woman, "You are a savage and a dangerous woman" and the woman replies, "I am speaking the truth. And the truth is savage and dangerous."

Courage is a heart word, but we must not conflate the soft and romanticized vision of the heart with the gritty, beating muscle that is the lifeblood of activism and peacemaking. Our call to courage is to find our voices, tell our own hearts, and to fight for the right and the space for all women and girls to do the same. And, as Maggie Kahn wrote, "Stand before the people you fear and speak your mind—even if your voice shakes." That is what it means to be bold.

INTRODUCTION

by Rachel M. Vincent

"It is time to stand up, sisters, and do some of the most unthinkable things. We have the power to turn our upsidedown world right." – Leymah Gbowee

When I was 10, I was an avid reader and particularly loved reading biographies. I vividly recall reading short, child-versions of biographies about Florence Nightingale—the nurse who pioneered the use of hygiene in field care and saved countless lives on the front lines during the Crimean War—and biographies of Sojourner Truth and Harriet Tubman, two African Americans who had bravely made their way from the South to the North to escape slavery. Harriet Tubman traveled mostly at night, and used moss—which grows on the side of the tree that gets the least amount of light, the north side—to guide her to freedom. To this day, while walking in the woods, I find myself checking on which side of the tree the moss is growing.

It is perhaps not surprising then that as I grew older, I sought out books written by and about women. In my turbulent teens and 20s, it was the lives and experiences of women I had never met—writers like Harper Lee, Sylvia Plath, Maya Angelou, Nawal El Saadawi, Gloria Naylor, Julia Alvarez and Arundhati Roy—who helped me to feel less alone in this world. Their collective wisdom pointed me towards a new kind of North, an interior freedom; they showed me that there are many ways in this world to be a woman, and that fear was normal, but so was boldly refusing to accept things as they are.

In 1983, when I was 18, my mother gave me a copy of Carol Gilligan's book, *In A Different Voice*. This book posited the theory, ground breaking at the time, that women and men have different approaches to morality. Gilligan's work has since been knocked off its pedestal, but the core idea that women and men have different "voices" and ways of being in this world has always stuck with me, and in ways big and small, has shaped my life.

Fast-forward more than 30 years. I now find myself working with six women Nobel peace laureates at the Nobel Women's Initiative. The Initiative's leader, Liz Bernstein, shares not only a passion for feminism and peace work with me, but also a deep love for the writing of women and women's stories. During human rights delegations to countries like South Sudan, Honduras, India and the Democratic Republic of the Congo, Liz and I fill time on planes or buses discussing books we love; back home in Ottawa, copies of books by her favourite writers—some of whom she has been corresponding with for years—start appearing on my desk.

This collection of intimate profiles about extraordinary women *by* other equally extraordinary women is the result of many such relationships. Award-winning writer Alexandra Fuller graciously agreed to write a profile of the late environmentalist and human rights leader Wangari Maathai because she and Liz had already had many long-distance conversations about Africa, where Fuller grew up, and where Liz worked on the International Campaign to Ban Landmines. When Liz moved to Canada, she sought out the work of Canadian women writers, including the gifted Madeleine Thien, who writes about Chinese activist Ding Zilin in this collection.

Not surprisingly, then, some of the stories and women in this book are interconnected. Peace activist and philanthropist Cora Weiss, profiled in this book by Iranian-British human rights activist Sanam Naraghi Anderlini, was also a mentor to Nobel peace laureate Jody Williams. And an organization that Cora led, the African American Students Foundation, brought young Wangari Maathai to the U.S. on a university scholarship in the early 1960s—more than 40 years before she won the Nobel peace prize.

Some of the women you will meet in these pages make it clear what it is to be a feminist. Scholar and writer Valerie M. Hudson explores how feminist icon Gloria Steinem has been working for a shift in foreign policy based on the feminist goal of peace. Iranian-American writer Azadeh Moaveni writes compellingly of how the life of Iranian human rights defender Shirin Ebadi demonstrates that there is no contradiction in being a feminist and Muslim. Other stories in this collection are about rediscovering our past. The memory of Charlotte Mannya Maxeke, known as the "mother of the black freedom" to many in South Africa, was almost lost until Zubeida Jaffer and other anti-apartheid activists reclaimed her story.

Several of these stories focus on the mother-daughter relationship or how mothers build movements to end violence. Native American activist and actor Casey Camp-Horinek lovingly introduces us to her mother, Jewell Faye McDonald, who fearlessly resisted assimilation into the dominant white culture. Canadian journalist Nahlah Ayed shares the story of French activist Latifa Ibn Ziaten, who turned the loss of her son into a powerful tool that helps young people walk away from extremism.

Some stories cut very close to the bone. Honduran activist Berta Cáceres—celebrated here by her daughter Laura Zúñiga Cáceres—was brutally assassinated in March 2016. This collection delves into the lives of other activists who have died in recent years, including Natalya Estemirova, who was targeted for her tireless work exposing human rights abuses in Chechnya.

Award-winning Russian journalist Anna Nemtsova says her work is an effort to honour Natalya, "the most courageous woman I will ever meet." These stories highlight not only the dangers involved in being a woman who dares to live boldly, but also demonstrate how the vision they had for the world lives on through other women.

Earlier I described the women in this book as "extraordinary." At the root of that word is "ordinary." Both the women writing and the women who inspire them are just like women you know. They are your mother, your sisters, your aunts; women in every community across this planet doing the hard, sometimes dangerous, and often lonely, work of challenging the status quo and responding to violence and injustice in its many forms.

I hope you see glimpses of yourself in some of the women you read about in these pages. Perhaps some of them will even inspire you to follow the metaphoric moss on the north side of the trees towards boldness.

CONTRIBUTING WRITERS

Louise W. Knight
Zubeida Jaffer
Casey Camp-Horinek
Julia Alvarez
Monia Mazigh
Rana Husseini
Elizabeth Abbott
Kathy Kelly
Sanam Naraghi Anderlini
Alexandra Fuller
Bopha Phorn
Valerie M. Hudson
Doreen Baingana
Marilyn Waring
Robi Damelin
Pamela Yates
Madeleine Thien
Audrey Wells
Lydia Cacho
Anna Nemtsova
Danai Gurira
Fiona Lloyd-Davies
Azadeh Moaveni
Laura Zúñiga Cáceres
Cindy Blackstock
Hooria Mashhour
Nahlah Ayed
Aja Monet

JANE ADDAMS

Born in 1860, Jane Addams was a peace activist, suffragist and an advocate for labour rights, civil rights and free speech. In 1919 she founded the Women's International League for Peace and Freedom, a women's movement to convince world powers to disarm and enter into peace agreements. She also co-founded Hull House, the first settlement house in the U.S., which provided poor people and immigrants with social, educational and artistic programs. In 1931, she became the first American woman to win the Nobel Peace Prize.

A TRUE PIONEER

By Louise W. Knight

I first encountered Jane Addams in a college course, when I was assigned to read her classic semi-memoir, *Twenty Years at Hull House*. That year I was living at the top of a house, in a room tucked under the eaves. Sitting on my bed—a mattress on the floor—the rain drumming on the roof above my head, I underlined passage after passage, mesmerized by her wise, thoughtful voice. Who *was* this woman?

In time I would learn a great deal about Jane Addams. My education on her life began soon after I graduated, when I read a new biography. The interpretation of what drove her seemed wrong to me. I found myself thinking, in the all-too-confident flush of frustration, that *even I* could write a better book than that! That seed of impatience turned into my first book, *Citizen: Jane Addams and the Struggle for Democracy,* published decades later. My book captured her journey from a childhood of privilege in northern Illinois to a chosen life among working people in an industrial neighborhood of Chicago, then traced her moral growth from a well-intentioned but naïve philanthropist into a skilled activist, fighting for a working people's agenda of labor rights, immigration rights, the vote for women, and peace.

My book ended in 1899, when she was 39 years old and on the cusp of what would become a deep and wide commitment to peace work. I took up her later life in my second book, *Jane Addams: Spirit in Action*, which was the first full-length biography of Addams published since the one I had read some three decades before. This volume covered both her early years and the story of her emergence as a leader in the American progressive movement and the world peace movement, achievements that led her to become the first American woman, and the second woman ever, to receive the Nobel Peace Prize.

I knew very little about the peace movement when I began to write the book. Although I was in college during the campus campaigns against the Vietnam War and the draft, I was an observer, not an activist. When I attended anti-war rallies, I stood at the back, listening as young men berated the government for fighting a pointless war. They were very angry. Their fury made me, an upper-middle-class young woman who had been raised to overvalue politeness, uncomfortable.

Another reason I did not understand the rallies was my gender. I realized, of course, that my male fellow students were, unlike me, required to register for the draft when they turned 18 and that, once they were out of school, they could be drafted into the military by a periodic government lottery. But I did not grasp how trapped they felt as they faced the possibility that the government would force them to fight or become draft dodgers and flee the country. I could not put myself in their shoes.

As for war itself, I had no clear ideas on the subject. On the one hand, I did not like war because it was violent and all about death. On the other hand, I found it hard to distrust the military since my father—so handsome in his uniform—had been a captain in the navy and served in World War II and the Korean War.

I gained a new perspective on war from studying Addams. In her twenties, her first interest was not in international relations but in interpersonal ones. Uncomfortable with anger—here was a bond we shared!—she was drawn to the Christian idea of nonresistance: the idea that no matter how one was treated, one should avoid responding with force. Though she was raised a Christian, and knew her Bible well, it was Leo Tolstoy's *My Religion* that converted her into a "nonresistant" or, as his followers were called—for he inspired a generation of nonresistants—a Tolstoyan. Tolstoy wrote that Christ taught "never do anything contrary to the law of love."[1] Inspired by this uncompromising vision, Addams adopted it as her own. She sought to be loving in all her relations and schooled herself to control her own fierce temper. In later years, she became famous for her unflappable and loving persona, but no one should doubt it was hard-earned.

Still, Addams was what we might call an "interpersonal" nonresistant until, in 1898, the United States went to war with Spain over Cuba and the Philippines. Stunned that her country was at war, Addams wrote a friend: "I will have to become more a Tolstoyan or less of one right off." Not one to avoid a moral dilemma, she dug deep into her soul and, at age 39, came out against the war. Calling peace a "rising tide of moral feeling," she urged that it should "engulf all pride of conquest and make war impossible."[2]

In the opening years of the 20th century, Addams became involved in the national peace movement and its annual congresses. These were mostly male affairs, whose proceedings were filled with the new century's smug assurance that the nations of Europe and North America were far too "civilized"

---

[1] Louise W. Knight, *Jane Addams: Spirit in Action* (New York: W. W. Norton, 2010), 54.
[2] Louise W. Knight, *Citizen: Jane Addams and the Struggle for Democracy* (Chicago: University of Chicago Press, 2005), 95.

ever to engage in the foolishness of war again. Addams was not so sure.

In a book she published in 1907 titled *Newer Ideals of Peace*, she expressed hope that war was a waning international force in the face of spreading democracy, but also examined how militarism permeated every aspect of American society. To her, the word's meaning included being willing to use physical force but also a belief in hierarchy. Militarism distrusted the people; saw enemies everywhere, whether overseas or around the corner; based a nation's patriotism on war; disdained immigrants; embraced an "unrestricted commercial spirit"; and distrusted women. And she defined peace to mean not just the absence of war but that which the spread of democracy made possible: "the unfolding of worldwide processes making for the nurture of human life."[3]

As I read *Newer Ideals*, I found that Addams, in her quietly revolutionary way, was teaching me, as she taught many others, to think about militarism differently—to see it as the dangerous and anti-democratic cultural assumption that the strong *should* dominate the weak.

When Europe erupted into war in 1914, Addams again faced a moral challenge squarely. After some effective grassroots organizing, she was elected president of the newly-formed Woman's Peace Party of the United States. She headed its delegation to the meeting at The Hague that gave birth to the International Committee of Women for Permanent Peace, later renamed the Women's International League for Peace and Freedom. Its platform urged the mediation of international disputes and called for women to have a part in debates and decisions about war and peace. The committee sent a delegation

---

[3] Knight, Spirit, 137, 139.

that included Addams to meet with officials of the warring nations and urge them to negotiate. Addams knew they had "one chance in ten thousand" of succeeding. But trying was what mattered. As she told the committee, "Social advance must be pushed forward by the human will and understanding united for conscious ends."[4]

Returning home, Addams was optimistic at first, having great faith in people's good judgment when given the facts. She and others in the Woman's Peace Party set out to educate Americans about militarism through a massive campaign of speeches, meetings and editorials. But the nation's mood switched in 1917, once President Wilson led the nation into the war and launched a powerful propaganda campaign to rouse support. After Addams gave a speech in which she defended the patriotism of pacifists, she was attacked in newspaper editorials across the country as a traitor, was booed in public, and later shut out of lecture halls. She sank into despair. Feeling cut off from her fellow citizens, she doubted herself. Was she wrong in her stance? In the end, she concluded that propaganda had undercut the people's judgment and that she had to be true to her conscience. She wrote, "A man's primary allegiance is to his vision of the truth and … he is under obligation to affirm it."[5]

Today, I know what drew me to Jane Addams. It was her moral courage. In her twenties, she transformed her comfortable but narrow life into a career of intense work that taught difficult lessons. Later she became a world leader in the almost impossible, but essential, task of working for peace. And in tracing her life, I learned why peace matters—that it constitutes the condition of freedom that nurtures the growth of the human spirit. Finally, in studying Addams, I found the shape I wanted my own activism to take: I am a biographer now, committed to

---

[4] Knight, Spirit, 201, 202. [or Ibid., 201, 202.]
[5] Knight, Spirit, 220. [or Ibid., 220.]

bringing to today's readers the stories of the morally courageous who are no longer alive but from whom we can learn. My hope is that someday, someone will read the first pages of a book I wrote, maybe underneath an attic roof thrumming with the sounds of rain, and think, "Who was this woman?" And keep on reading.

LOUISE W. KNIGHT is an American historian and author of two books about the life of Jane Addams: *Citizen: Jane Addams and the Struggle for Democracy* and *Jane Addams: Spirit in Action*. She is currently writing a book about the Grimké sisters, two American abolitionists and women's rights activists of the 1830s.

CHARLOTTE MANNYA MAXEKE

Charlotte Mannya Maxeke became her country's first black female university graduate in 1901, and eventually was known as the "Mother of Black Freedom" in South Africa. A talented singer, she performed throughout Britain and North America with a choir group, and completed her Bachelor in Science at Wilberforce University in Ohio. On her return to South Africa, she became a social activist, fighting for the rights of women and black South Africans, particularly the right to education.

MOTHER OF BLACK FREEDOM

By Zubeida Jaffer

L ike many black South Africans, I grew up without a sense of my history. When I was a student in the 1970s, it was against the law just to say Nelson Mandela's name. Many important black South Africans from the 20th century were written out of the "official" history, their stories erased or forgotten. Charlotte Mannya Maxeke was one of these figures. Highly influential in early women's movements, Charlotte fought to liberate black South Africans from the injustices of colonial rule around the turn of the century, and worked to provide a basic level of education for all. Yet until four years ago, I had heard her name only vaguely.

In 2012, the vice-chancellor at the University of the Free State, where I am writer-in-residence, asked if I would be interested in researching and writing Charlotte's story. The vice-chancellor was fascinated with Charlotte because she was the first black South African woman to graduate from university—in 1901, to be precise—a time when she'd not only have been denied entrance to *any* university in her country of birth, but when only a handful of white women were accepted to study in the U.S. When the vice-chancellor approached me, South Africa was already deeply involved in a movement to reclaim its authentic history. Charlotte—who'd already had a submarine and a hospital named after her—was clearly one of these stories, yet the public only knew of her superficially. They were largely unaware of the real scope and significance of her activism. I accepted the opportunity to write about Charlotte, never expecting she would have such a profound influence on my own life.

Charlotte's story begins with her beautiful singing voice, an instrument that cleared a path for her across the seas and helped her become the country's first black female graduate. Singing was part of family life for Charlotte and her siblings, and by the time she attended high school in Port Elizabeth in the 1880s, she already excelled in school choir competitions. After graduating, Charlotte continued to sing at church functions while working as a teacher in Kimberley. The town was in the heartland of the country's emergent diamond mines, which were chiefly exploited for the benefit of British colonialists. This was the period when the germs of race-based ideology took hold, a precursor of apartheid. Charlotte, with her intellectual circle, played an important part in resisting growing racism, injustice and inequality, although their work would then be forgotten for decades.

Charlotte loved books from an early age, a passion her parents bequeathed to her. She also recognized the importance of education as a great social equalizer. Even as a young girl, she was greatly concerned that most people in her father's village could not read, and decided to educate herself so that she could teach them one day. Charlotte dreamed of higher education after high school, but university in South Africa was not an option for a black woman at the end of the 19th century. It wasn't until an American musical group called the Virginia Jubilee Singers hit the shores of South Africa, taking Kimberley by storm, that Charlotte's dreams of higher education crystallized.

Charlotte learned from members of the Jubilee Singers that black people in the U.S. were fighting for their rights and had started universities where they could shape their own destinies. The news made her more determined than ever to continue her education. Inspired by the Virginia group, Charlotte and friends from her church started their own choir, and were eventually invited to America and Britain to tour, once even performing for Queen Victoria. Charlotte's trips abroad opened her eyes. In Britain, she met women of colour with professional careers and realized that this life, too, should be possible for herself and for other black women. "Let us be in Africa even as we are in England," she wrote for the prestigious London magazine *Review of Reviews*, when she was 22 and touring there. "Here we are treated as men and women. Yonder we are but cattle. But in Africa, as in England, we are human. Can you not make your people at the Cape as kind and just as your people here?"

While performing in the U.S., Charlotte succeeded in gaining entrance to Wilberforce University, in Ohio, where she completed a Bachelor of Science degree. At a time when the oppression of people of colour was institutionalized both in the U.S. and her native country, this was a truly remarkable feat. Her time at Wilberforce was formative. She studied with and under a number of eminent African Americans—such as the writer W.E.B. Du Bois—who were also involved in America's black protest movements. Inspired by the struggle in the U.S., Charlotte returned to South Africa to use some of the ideas she had been exposed to there to fight injustices in her own country.

Charlotte returned home during the Anglo-Boer War. Her family had relocated from Kimberley to her father's birthplace of Ramokgopa, and she joined them there. She took up a position in a women's organization within her church, the African Methodist Episcopal church, which she had introduced in South Africa. As in the U.S., the AME Church played an important role in fighting oppression. Charlotte's pivotal role in establishing this church in her homeland provided an important base for later work to improve social and gender relations.

Charlotte was determined to build schools and strengthen education for all black South Africans. She also became involved in opposing the unequal treatment of women in South African society. As the only female in a circle of highly educated men who were primarily interested in fighting the injustices of colonialism, Charlotte made herself heard both inside and outside this group. She was often invited to debate publicly on social matters, including women's rights, education or the rights of workers. During a public address in 1912, for example, she urged the Workers Union to allow women to become full members and be granted equal pay.

Her activism transcended colour and gender barriers. In 1921, she was invited to speak to an organization advocating for the voting rights of white women! In 1912, Charlotte had been the only woman present at the launch of the African National Congress—women weren't allowed to be voting members of the ANC until 1945. She wielded further influence by becoming president, in 1918, of the Bantu Women's League, a forerunner of the ANC Women's League and an organization that held great sway with politicians and legislators. While Charlotte was president, the Bantu League led the campaign to oppose "Pass Laws," which severely restricted the free movement of black South Africans within their own country.

Throughout Charlotte's career, education remained a primary interest. In 1908, she helped establish a school for black South Africans near Johannesburg, called the Wilberforce Institute for the African Methodist Episcopal Church. Near the end of her life in 1939, this school, along with many other efforts to strengthen education for black South Africans, was jettisoned by minority governments of the time. After securing the end of apartheid in 1994, however, the democratic government and the AME Church revived the school, which is now run entirely by black South Africans and African Americans. It's fascinating: by reopening her school and rediscovering our history through figures like Charlotte, we return to the ideas she championed so many years ago. As black South Africans, we must not rely on outside help but shape our own lives, tell our own stories and build our own institutions.

Increasingly, as I researched Charlotte's life story, her amazing self-reliance influenced my own outlook. About that time, I also came to realize that my journalist's training was essentially informed by British, American and Dutch points of view. The journalist 'heroes' I'd been taught to venerate were foreign— and male. I'd had a colonial education and I was heartily sick of it: I wanted my own heroines.

Charlotte came along at the perfect time. Her story and ideas convinced me that we must create our own institutions. Modelling ourselves after foreign systems and looking to foreign figures for inspiration, as we have done for the past 20 years, has not worked. Today, a vibrant movement led by students and other social organizations, seeks to do just this. Charlotte's work and ideas—written out of our history in a shameful way—are again an inspiring model for us.

Charlotte's example impelled me to write a book about her life, published earlier this year. Her story could not emerge at a more significant time for South Africa. Year 2016 marks the 60th anniversary of the women's march that took place on August 9, 1956, when more than 20,000 women marched to the Union Buildings in Pretoria to hand the prime minister signed petitions opposing the Pass Laws. This year also marks the 40th anniversary of the student uprising of June 16, 1976, in Soweto, when high school students protested the introduction of Afrikaans as the primary language of instruction in schools. It is also the 20th anniversary of the dramatic Truth and Reconciliation Commission, where South Africans shared some of their traumatic experiences of apartheid.

Charlotte and her reforming contemporaries made monumental efforts to lay the foundation for education and peacebuilding at every level. If Charlotte and her circle had been allowed the freedom to follow their reforming path, we would not need to expend so much energy and talent today unraveling years of exclusion and separation. Let us now have the courage to follow their lead in breaking down barriers and repairing our social fabric.

ZUBEIDA JAFFER is an award-winning South African author and journalist and who was active in the anti-apartheid and trade union movements, and has been at the forefront of action to ensure more diverse voices are included in South African journalism. Her most recent book, *Beauty of the Heart*, details the life and work of Charlotte Mannya Maxeke.

JEWELL FAYE MCDONALD

Jewell Faye McDonald was six years old when she was taken from her Ponca family and sent to a Bureau of Indian Affairs Boarding School in Oklahoma. When she returned to her community as a teenager, she was reintroduced to the customs, knowledge and traditions of her people, which she passed on to her six children, some of whom today are prominent Native rights activists and environmentalists.

SHE CHOSE TO WALK THE RED ROAD

By Casey Camp-Horinek

Red powdery earth, hot and silty, clung to their sweaty faces like sacred ceremonial paint. Locked inside the touring car, the four children were afraid even to cry. As the car door slammed shut, so, too, did a door on the world they had always known.

Jewell Faye McDonald was six years old when she was kidnapped and taken a hundred miles away to a Bureau of Indian Affairs boarding school. Life would never be the same for her and the other Ponca children who were forced to leave their grieving parents and relatives.

Going from White Eagle to Cantoma in Oklahoma was only a five-hour trip on that August day in 1920, but it may as well have been a trip to Mars. These strangely dressed white people who held them captive couldn't even communicate with them, and truly seemed to have swooped down from another planet. How could the children know how to prepare for the foreign world they were about to enter? A world cast in the image of an

American military school: uniforms, haircuts, hard shoes that rarely fit. Waking up in dormitory bunks to the bugle's blare and marching to the cafeteria to eat food that made them sick. No one spoke their language, no one cared if they cried—or even died, for that matter.

Even though they were battered emotionally, psychologically, culturally and certainly physically, they held tight to one another and the beautiful teachings of their Ponca People. They endured.

Jewell's true name was Mathethacha, and she was my mother. Born to Te son monthe and Mazhugashon on a cold day when the geese flew north, she was one of the youngest of 10 treasured children, and one of only four to make it to adulthood. Mathethacha's father had been only eight years old when the Ponca "trail of tears" happened. The U.S. government forced the Ponca to relocate from Nebraska to Oklahoma in 1877, an arduous journey taken on foot. Mathethacha's father was one of only 537 who survived the trek to the new territory the next year, through what the survivors called the "hot country."

Mathethacha was raised within the value system of the "Old Ways." Her family told her of the time Waconda reached down through the Thunder clouds and passed the Sacred Pipe to the Ponca People. Along with the Pipe came instructions about what ceremonies to hold dear. She was taught that Water is life and life is Water. That to honour the Earth and all living things is to honour oneself. She knew about the sweat lodge, the coming-of-age and naming ceremonies. She was taught when to plant the corn and the prayers that went with sowing seeds. Where to find medicine and food, when to harvest. Every day started and ended with a prayer. Every day was a gift to be cherished and used to the benefit of all. She was taught to be thankful, kind in word and deed, to be truthful, to care for others.

The careful nurturing of Mathethacha's mind, body and spirit was abruptly severed on the day that she was torn from the fabric of her Ponca Ways.

"Boarding school kind of made us schizophrenic," she told me one day. This was in her later years, when she was looking back at her life. "It felt like they wanted us to be something that we never could be, no matter what we did. We tried to talk like them, 'cause of course they would knock us around if we talked in Ponca. We had to dress like them, cut off our braids and pray in their churches, like Waconda wasn't good enough. Then they would send us back home for three months in the summer and our own folks seemed somehow different to us. We didn't fit in anywhere," she said. "It made us a little crazy, you know?"

Mathethacha stayed in boarding schools until she was 15. The last was the Chilloco Indian School, close to the Oklahoma-Kansas border. There Mathethacha felt like she had taken all she could endure. After the abuse inflicted upon her from the age of six, she could not tolerate one more unwarranted assault. When the history teacher walked up behind her and smacked her on the head with a book for no reason at all, it was too much. Mathethacha stood up (all five feet of her), snatched the heavy book from the teacher's hands and smacked her head in the exact same spot. That very day, she left the school and everything it stood for, including the violence, forever. The walk home, back to the good ways of her People, was 25 miles.

The rest of Mathethacha's teenage years were very healing. Her family was thrilled to have her home. Even though reservation life was confining and—by any modern standards, way below the poverty level—living was good. They grew huge community gardens. When the annual Ponca Celebration came around at the end of every summer, the People came together and shared all they'd grown, and dried the rest for winter. Hunting, fishing and wild crafting helped to sustain them.

Mathethacha learned a lot from her Mom, Aunties and Grandmothers. The Old Ways were "just life." She observed and participated in end-of-life rituals and watched, listened and danced when the women's ceremonies took place. Spirituality was intricately woven into everyday occurrences, from the smallest to the largest. As a People with strong oral traditions, paying attention and committing to memory were the norm. Mathethacha grew in ways that had sustained her People through every possible experience.

When Mathethacha was 19, she met and married Woodrow Howard Camp, a tall, intelligent young man from Pawhuska, Oklahoma. He learned to speak Ponca fluently and became aware of Ponca customs, relationships and cultural nuances. Their first daughter was born in 1936. Over the next three decades, my parents would have six children together, moving from place to place for work and facing the Great Depression and World War II together. They also lived through a new U.S. government-led relocation of our People, this one from the rural areas where the vast majority of us lived, into urban areas. The government offered money and training to "assimilate" the Ponca and other Red Nations Peoples into the big cities. I was the last of their children, born in Fresno in 1948. For 20 more years, the family chased jobs and dreams until the chop and change of life took its toll on their relationship and my Mother and Father parted ways.

A new curve in the circle of life brought Mathethacha home to White Eagle, Oklahoma in the early 1970s, with her second husband. Her days were spent with family. She submerged herself in the Ponca culture in every way. It felt good to speak her own language. It brought strength and healing to listen to the old Ponca songs and dance the ancient women's dances. After starting a long childhood journey away from her People in that dusty car, she was finally home for good.

My mother's unflinching strength in the face of every obstacle gave me strength and influenced my path in life. She instilled my need to give voice to the injustices that we encounter as Red Nation Peoples. I became an actress to dispel the "redskin image" created by Hollywood moviemakers. I spoke about our culture in public schools so my children could hold their heads high during false and biased history lessons. Sometimes, as a family, we participated in civil disobedience. As I aged, I began to wear the mantle of the Matriarch and share the messages of my ancestors, just as my mother did. Now that message is being shared from the very grassroots of my People all the way to the United Nations.

Mathethacha's sons and grandsons followed the warrior path of the ancestors as well. Her son, Carter Camp, led the American Indian Movement in the '70s and headed the Oklahoma delegation along the "trail of broken treaties" cross-country caravan in 1972 to Washington, D.C. Carter's brothers, Dwain and Craig, joined him in the Wounded Knee Occupation of 1973, when approximately 200 Ogala Lakota and followers of the American Indian Movement seized and occupied the town of Wounded Knee, South Dakota, on the Pine Ridge Indian Reservation. This town was where, in 1890, the U.S. army massacred or wounded hundreds of Lakota men, women and children. In 1973, Mathethacha's sons were among those calling out the government for failing to honour treaties with Native American people, and demanding renegotiations. The next chapter for our family would be environmental activism.

As a People who know and respect their connection with Mother Earth, active environmentalism is a natural progression. Mathethacha had taught her children and grandchildren that a warrior has a responsibility to protect and defend all life. The prayers and actions of our ancestors make our lives possible, and we must love, care for and safeguard one another and the

Earth for future generations.

Our Mother made her journey home to be with relatives in the Spirit World on April 27, 1999. We miss her every day, although she has left us with what seems like time-released messages from the other side. A year after Mom had made her transition, my family was sitting out on our back porch. We live five miles off the highway on a dirt road. No traffic, the nearest neighbour a mile away. Suddenly, we see an entire caravan of vehicles turning into our long driveway. Vehicles of every description, including wildly painted hippie buses and vans. They stopped, turned off their motors and started spilling out into our five-acre yard with tents and other camping stuff. We approached them in wonder.

It turned out that they were caravanning across the United States to promote PEACE ON EARTH, the slogan displayed brightly on the side of the largest bus. They hearkened from around the globe: Buddhist monks, friars, Quakers, people from Denmark, Mexico, Germany, Japan, Africa, Canada, Panama and across the U.S. We asked them who they were and what they were doing at our place. The leader of their group said, "We met your wonderful mother last year. She gave us directions and told us to come by and stay a week or so. She said that you guys would feed us and welcome us because of the message we're carrying."

Okay, Mom. We hear you, loud and clear. We are following you on that Sacred Red Road.

CASEY CAMP-HORINEK is a Native rights activist, environmentalist and actor from the Ponca Nation of Oklahoma. She is known for her work on such films as *Share the Wealth* (2006) and *Running Deer* (2013).

MIRABAL SISTERS

The Mirabal Sisters were four sisters from the Dominican Republic who led an opposition movement against the brutal dictatorship of Rafael Trujillo in the late 1950s. On November 25, 1960, three of the four sisters were murdered on orders from Trujillo. Their death sparked outrage across the country and eventually led to Trujillo's assassination. In their honour, the United Nations in 1999 designated November 25 as the International Day for the Elimination of Violence Against Women.

THE BUTTERFLY EFFECT

By Julia Alvarez

I owe my life to Las Mariposas. In a sense, we are all beneficiaries of their example. Had it not been for the wing beats of their activism, many of us would not be flying.

Las Mariposas was the code name of the Mirabal sisters, who were four young women who grew up in the Dominican Republic under the regime of Rafael Leonidas Trujillo, one of the bloodiest and longest-lasting dictatorships in the Americas. While occupying the country in the 1910s and 20s, the U.S. Marines trained Trujillo and then named him head of the National Army, which would set him up to later take control of the nation. In its bid to keep the hemisphere free of communism, the United States supported Trujillo for many years. It was the old foreign policy of "He's an S.O.B. but he's our S.O.B."—a policy that kept many repressive regimes in power throughout the southern Americas for decades.

The Mirabal sisters organized a widespread underground movement to bring democracy and freedom to their country. They became powerful symbols, inspiring many disaffected citizens to join the underground. This threat to the dictatorship could not be tolerated. On November 25, 1960, three of the sisters, along with the driver of their jeep, Rufino de la Cruz, were ambushed as they were returning home from visiting their jailed husbands. Their murder was the final blow. The people of the Dominican Republic, who had lived in fear, enduring oppression for 31 years, rose up and toppled the dictatorship.

The fourth sister, who had not been on the fateful ride, survived. Dedé Mirabal went on to raise her orphaned nieces and nephews and to become a force for truth-telling and reconciliation after the dictatorship. It was Dedé who opened a museum in her sisters' memory in the family home; Dedé who told the story of their activism and murder, over and over; Dedé who kept faith and bore witness, modeling to a broken, divided people how to forgive but never forget. For 54 years after their deaths, with unwavering energy and strength, Dedé Mirabal led the country out of its bloody past and toward the unfinished experiment of democracy her sisters and so many other victims had given their lives to attain.

When the Mirabal sisters were murdered in 1960, my parents, three sisters and I were newly arrived in New York. We had managed to escape with our lives. Before our abrupt departure, I had not known that my father was involved in the underground movement. When several members of his particular cell were arrested, my father knew it was just a matter of time before those captured began disclosing names under the brutal torture that Trujillo's secret police would inflict.

Once I learned their story, the Mirabal sisters had a powerful hold on my imagination. They were my shadow sisters, the ones who had stayed behind, the ones who did not get out, the three who had paid with their lives. I knew I had a debt to pay. But I didn't yet know how.

Growing up in the Dominican Republic, I had been raised in the traditional way of a 1950s Latin American female. Girls were not expected to get much of an education. We were to marry young, raise a family. Ours was primarily an oral culture, even more so because of the dictatorship. Being bookish branded you as a dangerous intellectual. (Minerva, the most revolutionary among the Mirabal sisters, was a reader.) I was very much a product of that upbringing: I hated school; I disliked reading; such solitary activities were a form of punishment to me. But my family was full of storytellers, amazing tale-spinners who could hold me spellbound.

When we arrived in the United States, I found myself suddenly bereft in a new language. My sisters and I encountered prejudice—bullies in the school playground who called us names and told us to go back to where we'd come from. I had to find a new homeland, and with the help of my teachers and librarians, I discovered books and the world of the imagination, where no one was barred. I no longer had my family of storytellers, but through reading I could access stories, and through writing them, share my own with others.

One of the first stories I felt compelled to tell was the story of the Mirabal sisters. On frequent trips back to the Dominican Republic, I began researching their lives, and in doing so, I met and established a special bond with Dedé, the surviving sister. Along with her orphaned nieces and nephews, I called her Mamá Dedé. She was the mother of my activist soul, the muse who inspired the novel I published in 1994 about her and her sisters, *In the Time of the Butterflies*.

The story of the Mirabal sisters began to spread. In 1999, the United Nations declared November 25 as International Day for the Elimination of Violence Against Women, in their honour.

Looking back, what I'm struck by is the fact that these young women, seemingly powerless, obviously vulnerable, managed to accomplish so much! Not only did they spark a national movement that eventually toppled a powerful dictator with his vast network of secret police and absolute control of all avenues of communication, but beyond the borders of one small nation, they went on to inspire an international movement, and become global symbols of freedom for women and men everywhere.

In her powerful book *Hope in the Dark: Untold Stories, Wild Possibilities,* Rebecca Solnit talks about the surprising and often indirect ways in which change happens. She calls it "the indirectness of direct action." We do one little thing, expecting a certain result right away, but what happens is beyond what we imagine, and not necessarily on our watch. One of the examples Solnit cites: a story told by a member of the Women's Strike for Peace, a small, hardy and committed group of mothers in the early 1960s who were among the first activists against the Vietnam War. This woman said she often felt foolish, picketing in front of the White House in all kinds of weather, with at most a dozen members. No one seemed to pay them much attention or care. She secretly wondered if they were wasting their time. But then, years later, she heard Dr. Benjamin Spock, who had become one of the most high-profile and effective activists against the war, say that the turning point for him was spotting a small group of women week after week in snow, rain, heat and cold, protesting at the White House. If they were so passionately committed, he thought, he should give the issue more consideration himself.

Often, such profound changes begin humbly, under the radar, in the guise of a story that enters the bloodstream of the imagination and begins to change the way we see the world. Through reading or listening to a story, we experience life through another point of view; the muscles of understanding, which are also the muscles of empathy and compassion, are exercised and strengthened.

As a 10 year old, I heard a story that changed me. Three decades later I wrote it down. Less than a decade later the

United Nations passed its resolution. On November 25th, women and men moved by the story of women they never knew, stand together to eliminate violence and bring peace and justice to their corner of the world. In chaos theory, "the butterfly effect" is a term that describes how a subtle change in conditions can bring about significant changes in a later stage of that system. One extra wing beat of a butterfly in Brazil today can trigger a tornado in Texas a few days later. This is true not just of environmental forces but also of peace. A small group of thoughtful, committed citizens can change the world, as Margaret Mead reminds us. This change can begin with one imagination, maybe yours, transformed by reading about women like the ones in this book.

JULIA ALVAREZ is a writer who was born in New York City to Dominican parents, and raised between the two countries. Her father, an activist who resisted the Trujillo dictatorship, was forced to flee to the U.S. with their family in 1960. In 1994 Alvarez published *In the Time of the Butterflies*, a novel recounting the story of the Mirabal sisters. She has written 22 books, including novels, nonfiction and works of poetry and stories for young readers of all ages.

FLORA MACDONALD

Flora MacDonald was a prominent Canadian politician and humanitarian. She was Canada's first female external affairs minister, and one of the first women to run a high-profile campaign for the leadership of a major Canadian political party. In 2007 she founded Future Generations, an organization that supports schools, health and farming projects in Afghan villages. She died in 2015.

A POLITICAL LIFE OF COMPASSION

By Monia Mazigh

I am Tunisian-born and I never for a moment thought that one day, a Canadian woman of Scottish ancestry would influence my life and help me to make crucial decisions. But Flora MacDonald was destined to cross my life and change it.

I first met Flora in the summer of 2003, in personally tragic circumstances. My husband, Maher Arar, a Canadian citizen who emigrated from Syria to Canada with his parents in the late 80s, was arrested in September 2002, on his way back from Tunisia, where we had been vacationing. His flight to Montreal was on a stopover in New York's JFK airport, when he was pulled aside by FBI agents, interrogated for hours, then shackled and taken to the Metropolitan Detention Center in Brooklyn. I was still in Tunisia with our five-year-old daughter and eight-month-old son, waiting for Maher's phone call telling me he'd arrived safely. That call never came.

After days of frantic phoning with family members and friends about Maher's whereabouts, I learned from Canadian officials that he had been arrested. Later, I found out why: the FBI suspected Maher was an Al-Qaeda terrorist.

My life changed forever. At first I was in shock, overwhelmed by the news. Not knowing what to do, I extended my stay in Tunisia for about three weeks, hoping this "mistake" would be quickly corrected. I was in denial, dreaming of a miracle. Then I received confirmation that American authorities had not only forcibly detained my husband but sent him to Syria, a country he hadn't set foot in since age 17. That day I knew I had to return to Ottawa.

An entirely new life awaited me. In no time at all, I'd become a single mother, with no job except defending Maher as an honest Canadian citizen, a good father, and the victim of a terrible injustice. Gradually, I became an activist with one seemingly impossible mission: to bring my husband back from a Syrian dungeon. I had no connections. I couldn't hire a prominent lawyer. I didn't have financial means. I was able to do just one thing: speak out.

Very few people listened at first. But slowly, more and more people grew outraged at how my husband was being treated. They spoke out too.

Flora MacDonald was one of the most important people to speak out with me. She was a board member of the International Civil Liberties Monitoring Group, an organization where I work today as national coordinator. Her name was first raised to me as someone who was uniquely qualified to help me. Flora was a former minister for Canadian external affairs with a strong interest and expertise in Middle Eastern affairs. Politicians from all parties respected her tremendously, and we thought she could strengthen a small delegation of Canadian civil society organizations scheduled to meet with American officials at the U.S. Embassy to plead for Maher's release.

On the very day of this meeting, I suffered a terrible disappointment. Originally, I was to be part of this delegation, but on the morning of our appointment, Alex Neve, the secretary general of Amnesty International-Canada, phoned to say the official who had agreed to meet us didn't want me present. My heart sank. I asked why. Alex hesitated, obviously embarrassed. "The official mentioned that your presence as the wife of Maher Arar will make the meeting emotional." I felt devastated and outraged at this unfairness, but swallowed my pride and told Alex to go ahead with the meeting for Maher's sake.

Fortunately, I met Flora MacDonald that same afternoon. Her hair was white. She was tall and thin, with sparkling blue eyes. She welcomed me in an office where we met before going to the U.S. Embassy, and treated me as if she'd known me for years. Her optimism helped to balance the fear and disappointment of that day.

"I know what I am going to say to the American officials," she told me. "I will remind them how Canada helped the Americans during the hostage crisis in Iran." She explained that in 1980, six American diplomats had escaped the hostage-taking at the American embassy in Teheran by seeking refuge in the Canadian embassy. Flora herself had authorized the issue of false passports and currency to help the Americans pose as Canadians and exit the country with Canadian staff. I knew a bit about the Iranian revolution and the hostage crisis, but I'd only vaguely heard about the operation, known as "the Canadian caper," which inspired the 2012 movie *Argo*.

I wondered that day, and later, too, why this courageous lady wanted to help me, and why she'd trust me, not knowing exactly who my husband and I were. I admired her. No wonder she'd had the guts to help the American diplomats! Twenty years later, she wanted to ask the U.S. to return the favour, on Maher's behalf. She understood that the best and highest politics was about cooperation between nations. The U.S. is a powerful country and yet, in a time of crisis, it needed Canada to help secure the safety of American citizens. Could Flora's reminder of this shared history pressure U.S. representatives to, in turn, pressure Syrian representatives for Maher's release?

We walked to the embassy together, but I had to stay outside with a small crowd of supporters and journalists while Flora and Alex went in to meet the American delegates. I sweated with heat and expectation as we waited... and waited. When Flora and Alex finally came out of the meeting, Flora smiled kindly. "They listened to us but they refused to take any action. They kept saying that Maher Arar is now in Syria and that there is nothing the U.S. can do for him." I felt so discouraged. But Flora's reassuring smile kept my hopes alive, then and for a long time afterward.

My husband was finally released—375 days after his arrest, and after the concerted effort of Flora and so many other new friends. He came back a zombie, like a man from the grave. A man with no words, just a terrible pain inside from accumulated humiliation and suffering. But with his release, something magical happened too. People wanted to listen; they wanted to hear Maher's story. Speaking out helped. It paved the road back to justice.

I kept in touch with Flora after Maher came back. I would meet her at events or hear about work she was doing in Afghanistan, but our paths didn't cross in a significant manner again until the spring of 2004. Alexa McDonough, another friend and a former leader of the New Democratic Party (NDP), asked me one day why I didn't run for politics. Her question surprised me but, in truth, I had always loved politics. I grew up listening to my father's endless political discussions with friends in which, later, I took part. But I had never joined a political party. But now Alexa's question had made me feel restless. Half of me wanted to plunge into political waters, while the other hoped to preserve my independence.

I asked family and friends for advice but grew even more undecided. Then I thought of Flora. Who could possibly give me better advice? She isn't biased. Although she had belonged to the now-obsolete Progressive Conservative Party, I knew she wouldn't try to convince me to run for one party or another.

We met at her apartment near the historic Rideau Canal. She was warm and engaging company, and showed me photos from Afghanistan and pieces of art she'd brought back from her travels throughout the world. Then we sat on the couch and talked about her years of experience in the House of Commons. Flora suggested that if I ran for office, I should choose three main points to focus on—what I planned to do as a politician. Flora asked me what those might be, but I wasn't yet ready to answer. She assured me I'd have lots of time to reflect, but that deciding on these points was essential.

On International Women's Day in 2004, I came to a community centre in Ottawa South, my decision made. I was going to run for the NDP in a riding where I was told I had no chance to win. *The Ottawa Citizen* even went so far as to call me a "token candidate." But Flora's words of wisdom kept me grounded: "choose three points and concentrate on your message." And I did: I told the voters I would focus on immigrant issues, on the recognition of immigrants' credentials to work in Canada, and on human rights.

One day soon after, in my campaign office, I met a middle-aged volunteer. This man was from Afghanistan and he was always smiling. He had trained as a lawyer but couldn't practice in Canada. He told me he wanted to go back to school to qualify. "Who is helping you?" I asked. "My big friend, Flora MacDonald, the friend of Afghanistan," he answered. I was thrilled to hear her name again in this context. Flora never stopped. She helped Afghanis in their own country as well as émigrés to Canada.

Last summer, I learned that Flora had passed away. I was so sad. She had helped me often and freely, without expecting anything in return. When I was trying to decide if I wanted to run for politics, she didn't force issues or decisions. She treated me as an equal. She had helped my husband without knowing him personally but she knew what Canada should be standing for—and she wanted to right wrongs through her actions.

So many women, like myself, are standing on the strong shoulders of Flora MacDonald.

MONIA MAZIGH is a Canadian activist and academic who first came to national prominence for her efforts to free her husband, Maher Arar, a Canadian engineer of Syrian origin who was illegitimately detained in a New York airport in 2002 and sent to a prison in Syria. He was eventually released without charge, and later received compensation and an apology from the Canadian government. Mazigh is currently the National Coordinator of the International Civil Liberties Monitoring Group.

NAWAL EL SAADAWI

Nawal El Saadawi is a prolific Egyptian author, playwright, human rights activist and physician, and one of the leading feminists of her generation. Her books, which often address feminist issues that are taboo in Arab societies, have regularly been banned in Egypt and other Arab countries. Her recent work on women's rights has focused on eliminating the widespread practice of female genital mutilation.

TELLING DANGEROUS AND SAVAGE TRUTHS

By Rana Husseini

I was 27 years old and had been a crime reporter for the *Jordan Times* for less than a year, when I heard a story that changed my life. A 16-year-old girl named Kifaya had been raped and impregnated by a brother, then dared to divorce the much older man she'd been forced to marry, and was then killed by another brother to restore the family "honour." I learned that perhaps one-quarter of the women murdered in my country were victims of similar violence, so-called "honour crimes." Their killers were barely punished, and no one was speaking out. Over the next decade, both in newspaper stories and in my book *Murder in the Name of Honour*, I worked to break the silence surrounding a crime that claimed the lives of thousands of women every year, not only in my country but also around the world.

Kifaya's story inspired me, but the courage to be an activist, the need to speak the truth, and the belief that I could and must do so, had been born in me years before, when I first read the great Egyptian feminist Nawal El Saadawi.

I bought El Saadawi's revolutionary work *The Hidden Face of Eve* in 1984, when I was 17. I wasn't a feminist then, or even a very serious person. I was a student and played basketball and team handball for Jordan's women's national teams. Sports and getting a degree were my focus. But the book shocked me and opened my eyes. In my culture—even in my own educated, open-minded family—subjects like rape, prostitution, women's bodies, sexuality and sexual desire were not discussed. And in those days before the Internet, we had no other access to this forbidden information. Yet here was an Arab woman, writing in Arabic, graphically and angrily, about all these things and more: our culture's obsession with virginity and the punishment of those deemed to be "impure." The patriarchal nature of religion. Female genital mutilation, which was then nearly ubiquitous in Egypt, and which El Saadawi herself had suffered at age six: "The pain was not just a pain, it was like a searing flame that went through my whole body. After a few moments, I saw a red pool of blood around my hips."

I thought, "What a work! What courage to face an entire society!" The book grabbed my attention and my soul. It would be over a decade before I met El Saadawi in person, but she became my hero right there and then.

Nawal El Saadawi is a towering figure in Arab feminism, a woman of talent, drive and passion, who wrote that even as a girl she "would not believe in a country which robbed me of my pride and freedom, in a husband who did not treat me as an equal." She was born in a small village in 1931, one of nine children, and defied gender convention from the start. Expected to be a child bride, she got rid of one potential husband by blackening her teeth and clumsily spilling coffee on him. Later, she married and divorced three other men. El Saadawi went to university, trained as a psychiatrist and became an extremely successful doctor who founded the magazine *al-Sihha* (Health); at age 32, she became the director general of public health for the Egyptian Ministry of Health. During those years she also published three novels and short story collections. By then, her fury at the suffering she witnessed in her female patients pushed her toward writing nonfiction. In 1972, she became one of the first to publicly denounce female genital mutilation in her book *Women and Sex.*

El Saadawi paid dearly for daring to break the silence and speak up. Her book was banned, *al-Sihha* closed, and she lost her ministry of health position. But she did not stop. For her, feminism was all-encompassing, the only possible lens through which to see the world. "It is social justice, political justice, sexual justice," she said. "The link between medicine, literature, politics, economics, psychology and history." Next came the novel *Woman at Point Zero*, about a prostitute who goes to jail for murdering her pimp. *The Hidden Face of Eve* (also banned in Egypt) came out in 1977. In 1981, El Saadawi founded the Arab Women's Solidarity Association, edited the feminist journal *Confrontation*, and was arrested by the government of Anwar el-Sadat, along with around 1,500 other political dissidents. Denied pen and paper in jail, she befriended another inmate, a prostitute, who smuggled her an eyebrow pencil and toilet paper, on which she wrote a new book, *Memoirs from the Women's Prison.* After her release, her continued outspokenness brought death threats, and she was forced to flee the country. Yet El Saadawi was undaunted. "Danger has been a part of my life since I picked up a pen and wrote," she later said. "Nothing is more perilous than truth in a world that lies."

In exile, El Saadawi taught at universities in the United States and Europe, lectured and continued to write. Ultimately she authored 19 novels and short story collections, three plays, six works of memoir, and 10 of nonfiction. She never softened her approach. Words, she later wrote, should not "seek to please, to hide the wounds in our bodies, or the shameful moments in our lives. They may hurt, give us pain, but they can also provoke us to question what we have accepted for thousands of years." With her global reach, she inspired countless younger activists. She once told an interviewer she received 10-15 letters a day from women—like me—whose lives she touched. She refused to mellow with age. "I have noticed that writers, when they are old, become milder," she told one interviewer. "But for me, it is the opposite." In 1996, she returned to Egypt after years of exile; in 2011, at the age of 80, her fist raised and her thick hair wild, she marched with millions of young protesters in Cairo's Tahrir Square.

As a teenager, reading El Saadawi emboldened me. I thought "If this woman can speak up, so can I." Many years later, at a bookshop, I saw a new El Saadawi work, *My Life*. I thought "What new, daring material could El Saadawi provide this time?" I immediately bought the book—and once again, the bold and rebellious El Saadawi managed to shock me, and force me to think beyond traditional ideologies. She wrote of the pain and pleasure of her childhood, about love, lust, sex, marriage, divorce, becoming older and reconciling with oneself. One sentence made me smile bitterly: "I was a virgin at 20 when I got married following a big love story, that ended when I was 26 still a virgin, then I became a virgin mother and finally I was liberated by divorce." Even a powerful woman like El Saadawi could not make marriage work.

El Saadawi, along with other brave feminists like the late Fatema Mernissi of Morocco and Taslima Nasrin of Bangladesh, also gave me courage after the publication of my book on honour killings. I had broken a taboo, and was denounced as anti-Islam, anti-Jordan, anti-family, a Western collaborator, someone who was encouraging adultery and premarital sex. One man wrote me to let me know that he was cleaning his hunting rifle; another threatened to "visit" me if I didn't stop writing. But I knew that what I was doing was right, and that I could make a difference. With other young people, I formed the National Jordanian Committee to Eliminate Crimes of Honour, and I have seen enormous changes as the result of our work. The issue of so-called honour killing is no longer hidden in Jordan; it is now discussed in the press, and by citizens, government officials and others. The government has opened a reconciliation house to help abused women and children and there have been important changes in the way our judiciary handles such crimes. Punishments are harsher and the criminal court has designated a special tribunal to try these cases. Many other countries have begun to recognize and address the problem.

I am 49 now, and young girls sometimes tell me that my willingness to discuss something no one else would means something to them. I like to think I am passing on the strength that El Saadawi gave to me. The violence that still occurs daily against women and children is not something one can choose to talk about today, then forget about tomorrow. The week I wrote this essay—almost a half century after the publication of El Saadawi's *Women and Sex*—a 17-year-old girl died while undergoing an illegal genital mutilation procedure at a private hospital in Egypt.

In 2000, then again in 2015, I had the privilege of meeting my hero in person. We both spoke at the same conference and spent time together over a picnic in a local park. I was able to tell El Saadawi how important her books were to me, and to hear her express appreciation for my work. She is as vivid in person as she is on the page—funny, sarcastic, and boldly intelligent.

In many ways, it has become harder for feminists in our region. More conservatives are speaking out and extremist ideologies are spreading. El Saadawi's willingness to criticize religion and the wearing of the hijab has made her more controversial than ever. She remains fiercely herself. At one of the conferences where we met, a group stood outside the door handing out brochures that called El Saadawi a liar. Their actions did not bother her or change what she said.

One of my favorite El Saadawi quotes is from the novel *Woman at Point Zero*, when authorities say to a character "You are a savage and dangerous woman," and the woman replies, "I am speaking the truth. And the truth is savage and dangerous."

El Saadawi might well have been writing about herself.

RANA HUSSEINI is a reporter and human rights activist whose 2009 book *Murder in the Name of Honour* brought so-called crimes of honour to national attention in her native Jordan. She is a reporter with *The Jordan Times,* and a board member of Equality Now, an international human rights organization dedicated to women's rights.

JANE GOODALL

Jane Goodall is one of the world's leading primatologists. Her work in the 1960s revolutionized our understanding of chimpanzee behaviour, and challenged traditional research methodology. She now travels the world speaking about conservation and animal rights, and is the founder of the Jane Goodall Institute, which seeks to improve global understanding of great apes and help protect their habitat.

A WOMAN'S PLACE IS IN THE FOREST

By Elizabeth Abbott

I didn't grow up knowing about Jane Goodall, the British woman who, in changing the way scientists understood primates, redefined humans. Goodall first came into my life in 1963 through her article "My Life Among Wild Chimpanzees," published by the *National Geographic Society*, which generously sponsored her fieldwork and expected an in-depth article illustrated by superb photographs in return. Goodall's article introduced the world to a young woman fulfilling her childhood dream of watching wild African animals in their free state. Surprisingly, Goodall had not been a science prodigy at school, but rather, an enthusiastic nature lover and avid reader inspired by literature: Hugh Lofting's *Dr. Dolittle*, Rudyard Kipling's *The Jungle Book* and Edward Rice Burroughs' *Tarzan of the Apes,* the story of a British boy lost in the jungle and adopted by a female ape. "I wanted to come as close to talking to animals as I could," she later explained.

In 1957, during her dream trip to Kenya to observe "free, wild animals living their own undisturbed lives," Goodall met and so impressed the famous anthropologist and paleontologist

Dr. Louis Leakey that he hired her to assist on his projects, thereby enabling her to devote her life to studying chimpanzees. But following the wild chimpanzees of the Gombe Stream Chimpanzee Reserve in Western Tanzania was hard, tedious work. Goodall eventually won their acceptance and later, their trust. She documented incidents that astonished scientists, such as chimps hunting bush pigs and colobus monkeys for meat, thus disproving the belief, then widely held, that chimps are vegetarians.

Chimps making tools to extract and scrape termites from their mounds and into their mouths was another revolutionary discovery. Toolmaking was previously assumed to be an exclusively human activity. As Jane's patron, Louis Leakey, famously announced: "Now we must redefine tool, redefine Man, or accept chimpanzees as humans."

Predictably, Jane's detractors accused her of anthropomorphism: the scientific sin of attributing human characteristics to animals. But Jane knew better. "I had a marvelous teacher in animal behaviour throughout my childhood—my dog, Rusty," she declared. Jane knew that even if Rusty had been called "number 951" (before Jane, study chimpanzees were assigned numbers rather than names to maintain "objectivity"), he would have taught her the same truth.

Jane's scientific achievements were so impressive that Cambridge University admitted her as a Ph.D. student even though she had no undergraduate degree. She persevered in the university's discouraging and difficult ambiance, and on February 9, 1966, was awarded her doctorate in ethology—the study of behaviour—a field she had never heard of when she began her graduate studies. ("Is there such a word as ETHOLOGY?" she had asked her mother. "I feel it may be a misprint for ecology.")

Now an acknowledged scholar, Jane continued her work. She documented rival chimpanzee groups fighting, often to the death, which debunked the myth that chimps were peaceful creatures. She described how Passion and Pom, a mother-daughter duo, committed "barbarous murder" and then ate rival chimps' infants and concluded that, like their human relatives, chimpanzees have "a dark side to their nature." But she also observed acts of real compassion and, on one occasion, a joyous dance that she interpreted as an expression of awe at the sight of spectacular waterfalls, a response she likened to a religious experience.

Jane's impact on scholarly fieldwork methodology—acknowledging chimps as distinct individuals and naming rather than numbering them—was groundbreaking, and set a new research standard. Her development of a data-rich, scientific methodology that is both descriptive and analytic has been another major achievement, for it has allowed fine scientists, many of them women, to continue in her footsteps and advance research work.

When I was a younger woman, a doctoral student and a historian-in-the-making, I was also keenly interested in Jane's personal life. I was especially curious about how she managed to make her marriage to filmmaker Hugo van Lawick work, and to parent their son, Hugo (aka Grub), in the loving but unorthodox way she did, while also pursuing her research mission. After a decade together, Jane and van Lawick, who was depressive and dependent, divorced amicably. A year later, she married her lover, Derek Bryceson, a member of Tanzania's parliament and director of the country's national parks.

In my later years, after reading Dale Peterson's splendid biography *Jane Goodall: The Woman Who Redefined Man,* I better understood why she had not entirely succeeded in balancing her personal and working life, even with Bryceson. "Please try to understand that, whilst I may get a bit tired, I'm doing this because I LOVE it, and WANT to do it," she pleaded in one letter. "Please understand. Dearest, dearest, dearest Derek. I don't WANT to be stopped from doing this work...." Bryceson's love was so jealously possessive that Jane realized marriage to him was untenable. Death, not separation, ended this relationship, however, after Derek was stricken with metastatic cancer and died months later, with Jane at his bedside.

In November 1986, the Chicago Academy of Sciences' "Understanding Chimpanzees" symposium introduced Jane's new book, *Chimpanzees of Gombe: Patterns of Behavior*. This forum was also life-changing, for it transformed her from a research scientist into an advocate for conservation and education. Fellow scientists reported that forests were disappearing everywhere, and asked what good came of understanding chimpanzees when habitat destruction, logging, the bushmeat trade, illegal export and poaching were decimating these animals? Jane took on the role of chair of the newly formed Committee for Conservation and Care of Chimpanzees and became a peripatetic advocate and ambassador for chimpanzees, both wild and incarcerated, in research labs and zoos.

As Jane traded life in Gombe for one taken up with international airports, lobbying and countless speaking engagements, our worlds began to coincide. By then I too was an advocate for animals and the environment, and various newspapers had asked for reviews of Jane's books. The two that struck me most powerfully were *Reason for Hope: A Spiritual Journey* (1999), and *Hope for Animals and Their World: How Endangered Species Are Being Rescued from the Brink* (2009). Like me, Jane has despaired as humans persist in recklessly destroying world environments. But while humans are capable of evil "immeasurably worse than the worst aggression of the chimpanzees," Jane also believes that innate goodness co-exists with aggression. In the wise and moral choices and actions of individuals and groups, she sees the tools for change and regeneration. Everyone, she believes, can and should do something to help. Most impressively, she has founded Roots & Shoots, a hands-on, youth-led program providing young people with the knowledge, tools and inspiration they need to improve environments and quality of life, both human and animal.

A decade later, with a sixth mass extinction looming and the life of the planet at stake, Goodall gambles that she will, because she must, galvanize a critical mass of humanity to take action rather than merely wring their hands. *In Hope for Animals and their World,* she lists four saving graces: "Our quite extraordinary intellect, the resilience of nature, the energy and commitment of informed young people who are empowered to act, and the indomitable human spirit." Goodall's suggestions are supremely practical. The book's extensive appendix, "What You Can Do," includes pages of programs and websites that guide readers to "Take Action" and "Meet the Species." Young people, so crucial to future success, can participate in Roots & Shoots humanitarian and environmental programs.

Now in her eighties, Goodall travels three hundred days a year, advocating for forest conservation, sustainable development and the humane treatment of animals. A decade ago, I had the great good luck to meet her. She wore a simple sweater and slacks, her silver hair loosely tied back in a low ponytail, just as she'd worn it in the Gombe forests. I was one of a horde of admirers lined up to greet her. When my turn came, she smiled as I thanked her on behalf of the animals and quickly moved on to the next person. I wish now that I had been able to tell her how much she has inspired me in what matters most to both of us: protecting animals and world environments. "Take action!" she always urges, and in my own way, I have. My latest venture, candidacy for the Animal Alliance/Environment Voters Party of Canada in the 2015 federal election, was inspired by her example of lobbying and advocating rather than working directly with animals (which I, too, would much prefer).

In April 2002, Jane was named a United Nations Messenger of Peace and pledged to promote this message: "To achieve global peace, we must not only stop fighting each other, but also stop destroying the natural world." She guides us in her lectures, writings and personal engagements, and especially through Roots & Shoots, which has exploded from 12 original students in Tanzania to over 150,000 members in 130 countries.

As she roams the globe, reaching out to everyone she can, Goodall never ceases to remind people of their personal responsibility to make changes that matter, such as consumer and lifestyle choices and actions. She brings a stuffed monkey, and sometimes a rock from the South African prison quarry where anti-apartheid leader, Nelson Mandela, laboured for decades, to help make these appeals.

Jane's work has taught me that peacemaking is much more than simply opposing war. True peacemaking includes working to eradicate the root causes of war, especially the environmental degradation that triggers so many of the worst conflicts. Her lessons guide my life. Every little thing I do can count. I must be aware of what my choices entail, and always try to make the right ones for our shared world.

ELIZABETH ABBOTT is an award-winning Canadian writer and historian with a particular interest in women's issues, the welfare of animals, and the environment. Her most recent book, *The History of Marriage* (2010), is the final in a trilogy about human relationships.

MAIREAD MAGUIRE

After three of her sister's children were killed during the violence between Catholics and Protestants in Northern Ireland, Mairead Maguire organized massive demonstrations and other actions calling for a nonviolent end to the conflict. Along with Betty Williams, she is the co-founder of Peace People, and together the two women won the Nobel Peace Prize in 1976. She has spent her life since then standing in solidarity with people living in conflict, including in Palestine, Afghanistan and, most recently, Syria.

BEARING WITNESS TO INJUSTICE

By Kathy Kelly

At some point in the early 1990s, Burmese activists opposed to Burma's military government—which seized power in 1988—had invited Mairead Maguire to speak at a public event in Chicago. Several friends and I heard about her visit, and decided to try and meet her as she arrived at O'Hare airport. We hoped she would sign our petition calling for the Amoco Oil Company to stop supporting the Burmese regime, with its well-documented human rights abuses. Mairead's genuine warmth melted our initial apprehension about approaching a Nobel peace laureate who wasn't expecting us. Smiling broadly, she assured us that we all must hold vigils, work for justice, and of course get to know the Burmese population living in Chicago. She invited us to a sumptuous meal prepared by her Burmese friends.

From that earliest encounter, I have never doubted Mairead's genuine offer of friendship. Why wouldn't we choose peace and nonviolence together, and work to abandon war and militarism once and for all?

In the ensuing decades, whether writing to Mairead from a

federal U.S. prison—where I've spent lots of time locked up for participating in nonviolent protest actions—or talking to her in person about the possibilities of travelling to a war zone, I have always felt extremely fortunate to count on her warmth.

Certainly the Burmese people who welcomed her to Chicago on that day we first met understand how extraordinarily close she is to the struggles they have endured. Mairead, like many of them, has lost people she loved to conflict and also knows the anguish of waiting for loved ones to be released from prison.

***

On August 10, 1976, Northern Ireland was on the brink of civil war. One of Mairead's younger sisters, 31-year-old Anne, was walking with her four children to a local library in Belfast, when Joanne (eight), John (two-and-a-half), and Andrew (six weeks) were killed. "There was a clash between an active service unit of the Irish Republican Army and the British army," Mairead recalls. "The army shot dead the IRA man driving a getaway car. The car went up on the footpath and killed three of my sister's four children. She became dangerously ill and was not expected to live. I spoke out then against all violence. We started what became known as the Peace People, a movement committed to nonviolence and to social and political change."[1]

In the weeks and months that followed, Mairead, with Betty Williams—a peace activist who was an accidental witness to the killing of Mairead's niece and nephews—and Ciaran McKeown—a correspondent working with the *Irish Press*—worked constantly, often to the point of exhaustion. They organized tens of thousands of people from across Northern

---

[1] Maguire, Mairead Corrigan, Interview with Amitabh Pal. *The Progressive*, (April 2013) http://old.progressive.org/mairead-maguire-interview

Ireland in rallies that expressed the widely held desire to stop the bloodshed, imprisonments, torture and killings wracking Ireland, North and South. At one point they brought 35,000 people into the streets of Belfast to call for peace between the Republican and Loyalist factions.

Mairead's sister, Anne, her legs and pelvic bone broken, emerged from a coma after two weeks, and learned only then what had happened. She would take her own life four years later. Mairead recalls: "One of Anne's first outings was to the Falls Road rally in Belfast, where she stood before thousands of people and read the Declaration of the Peace People."[2] Anne also went to visit Mrs. Lennon, the mother of 19-year-old Danny Lennon, the IRA man who was killed driving the getaway car. "She has lost her child too," Anne said.[3]

It was for their work to end such suffering that Mairead and Betty Williams were awarded the 1976 Nobel Peace Prize. Mairead has lived up to this honour, working ever since to help people abandon violence and look for practical ways to come together, discard long held dogmas, and make difficult changes.

Shortly after she received the Nobel Peace Prize, Adolfo Pérez Esquivel, an Argentinian human rights activist, invited Mairead to visit Argentina. Mairead's colleagues encouraged her to accept the invitation, believing she could make a positive difference in the lives of student activists protesting the dictatorship of Carlos Menem. At first Mairead declined, saying that her role was to work closer to home, where she understood the circumstances and knew the people involved. But she eventually decided to go and, once there, met with young men

---

[2] Maguire, Mairead Corrigan, *The Vision of Peace: Faith and Hope in Northern Ireland*, Edited by John Dear. Eugene, OR: Wipf and Stock, 1999, p. 22

[3] Ibid., p. 23

and women whose classmates had been tortured, imprisoned and disappeared. The trip brought about the release of several student activists, and in 1980, nominated by Mairead, Adolfo Pérez Esquivel was awarded the Nobel Peace Prize for his work promoting nonviolent solutions to political trouble in Latin America. Mairead and Adolfo continue to work together, pressing for just and nonviolent solutions wherever people suffer human rights abuses.

In 1996, a small group of American activists meeting in my kitchen initiated a campaign to defy economic sanctions against Iraq. The sanctions—which the U.N. Security Council imposed four days after Iraq's invasion of Kuwait, in August 1990—were brutally punishing the most vulnerable people in Iraq, including the elderly and children. Iraqi children were suffering from malnourishment and gastrointestinal and respiratory diseases, but doctors couldn't treat them because Iraq was prohibited from buying needed medicines. Our group organized over 70 delegations to visit Iraq, carrying duffel bags filled with medicines and medical relief supplies for delivery to children and families. We called ourselves "Voices in the Wilderness," and Mairead was one of our strongest supporters. The U.S. government immediately threatened us with 12 years in prison and huge fines for violating the sanctions. We assured authorities that we understood the penalties but couldn't be governed by unjust laws that punished children. We then invited the government to join our effort. The sanctions, which lasted 13 years, directly contributed to the deaths of thousands of children under the age of five.

Mairead accepted our invitation to join a delegation sponsored by the Fellowship of Reconciliation, and invited her friend and fellow Nobel laureate, Adolfo Pérez Esquivel, to travel with her to Iraq. I had organized meetings with a diverse group of Iraqi citizens, but Adolfo, reading the itinerary, was puzzled and disappointed. Where were the young people? He and Mairead have always sought the earnest and unpressured viewpoints of young people wherever they travel. We swiftly arranged for a meeting with Iraqi girls studying in a Baghdad secondary school. One young woman stood and said: "You come and you say, you will do, you will do, but nothing changes. Me, I am 16. Can you tell me what is the difference between me and someone who is 16 from your country? I will tell you. Our emotions are frozen. We cannot feel!" The girl sat down, tearfully, while her friend stood and told us about the hunger faced by the students and their families, after a decade of bombings and economic sanctions. Testimony like this demonstrates why Mairead and Adolfo are right to insist we listen to the voices of the people who bear the brunt of rich governments' invasions and sieges—and why it is especially important to listen to young voices.

Mairead's commitment to listening has compelled her to join people in excruciatingly difficult situations. Once, after visiting imprisoned American peace activist Phil Berrigan, she felt it impossible to simply leave him and return to a comfortable life. The second Iraq war was approaching and the stakes for humanity ran high. Mairead refused to leave the prison. Prison guards strip-searched her, and put her into a cell. "I will never forget my short stay in that tiny, dirty, cramped, holding cell," Mairead later wrote. "It is incredible to think that one and a half million people, the entire population of Northern Ireland, are in American prisons and jails. The whole system is geared to dehumanize, control and weaken fellow human beings. Prison does not solve any problem. I wonder when the world's governments will begin to fight crime at its roots, by ensuring justice for the poor?"[4]

For over a decade, Mairead has borne witness to the nonviolent resistance movement in Israel and Palestine. She has regularly

---

[4] Maguire, *The Vision of Peace*, p. 95

accompanied nonviolent demonstrators in Bil'in, a Palestinian village in the central West Bank. During one such demonstration in 2007, Israeli Defense Forces shot Mairead in the leg. Six Palestinians were killed the next day, including a 17-year-old girl.[5] Three years later, Mairead travelled aboard the *Rachel Corrie,* a boat carrying a group of peace activists attempting to break the Israeli siege of Gaza by transporting humanitarian relief supplies to the people of Gaza. Israeli Defense Forces boarded the boat in international waters, arresting everyone. Mairead was deported and banned from entering Israel for 10 years.

Mere months later, when Mairead returned to Israel as part of a peace delegation with a fellow Nobel peace laureate, Jody Williams, Israeli authorities refused to allow her into the country, and detained her in Tel Aviv's Ben Gurion Detention Center. When Israeli security forces tried to deport her the following day, Mairead peacefully plunked herself down on the tarmac beside the plane. The crew refused to participate in forcing Mairead on board and demanded due process. After seven days in solitary confinement, Mairead appeared before Israel's Supreme Court. She told the court that she did not recognize her deportation order because the *Rachel Corrie* had gone to Gaza to end illegal and lethal collective punishment, and had been hijacked in international waters. The three judges upheld the deportation order, but Mairead's point was made. "Because I am critical of the Israeli government policies does not make me an enemy of Israel or her people," Mairead stated, "but an upholder of an ethic of human rights and nonviolence, and a believer that peace is possible between both peoples when justice reigns."[6]

---

[5] Dear, John, "Nobel Laureate Mairead Maguire Practices Nonviolence in Palestine," *National Catholic Reporter,* May 1, 2007 http://ncronline.org/blogs/road-peace/nobel-laureate-mairead-maguire-practices-nonviolence-palestine

[6] Peace People Press Release, Indymedia Ireland, 8th October, 2010. http://www.indymedia.ie/article/97884

Mairead believes that all people must ask how we can learn to live together and solve problems without killing one another. She insists the poorest in our world should be our top priority. "Perhaps the greatest tribute we can pay to Gandhi," she says, "is to work to eliminate poverty from the face of the earth. Gandhi said that poverty is the worst form of violence."[7]

In 2010, Voices for Creative Nonviolence activists began visiting with young Afghans. We were inspired by the work of Gandhi, Dr. Martin Luther King and Mairead Maguire. Mairead graciously agreed to join a Voices for a Creative Nonviolence delegation to Afghanistan. When she arrived in Kabul in December 2012, the young Afghan peace volunteers who met her at the airport were amazed as she hugged armed soldiers assigned to airport checkpoints. But this warmth is at the heart of her message: her exuberant recognition of every person's worth and her insistence that "the real enemies of humankind are disease, hunger, homelessness, poverty, greed, torture and war."[8] Mairead's action inspired the young volunteers to start a campaign to abolish war. Since that time, she has continually encouraged these young Afghans to build a "border-free" world, even as they bear the pressures of living in a war zone.

I remember how Mairead embraced our small group of peace activists in Chicago so long ago. We saw her beautiful capacity to make caring seem ordinary and something we can all do. Throughout my long friendship with Mairead, I have witnessed firsthand her intense desire to bring people from different groups together to seek truth and reconciliation. A core principle of nonviolence says "the means you use determines the end you

---

[7] Dear, "Nobel Laureate Mairead Maguire Practices Nonviolence in Palestine"
[8] Maguire, *The Vision of Peace*, p. 116

get." Mairead's unfailing courage and kindness is showing us the way.

KATHY KELLY is an American pacifist and highly acclaimed peace activist, one of the founding members of Voices in the Wilderness and is the co-coordinator of Voices for Creative Nonviolence. She has travelled to Iraq 26 times, including combat zones during the early days of both U.S.-Iraq wars, and her most recent travel focuses on Afghanistan and Gaza, along with domestic protests against U.S. drone policy. She has been arrested more than 60 times at home, and abroad, and in 2000 was nominated for the Nobel Peace Prize by the American Friends Service Committee.

CORA WEISS

Cora Weiss is President of the Hague Appeal for Peace, an international network dedicated to the abolition of war and making peace a human right. An activist since the 1950s, Weiss' work has included breaking race barriers in the 1960s, a leadership role in the anti-Vietnam war movement, convening women peacemakers during the Cold War and, in 2000, helping realize the historic United Nations Security Council Resolution 1325 that recognizes the essential role of women as peacebuilders.

WHEN THE CAUSE IS RIGHT

By Sanam Naraghi Anderlini

I'm fortunate to call Cora Weiss my friend and mentor, role model and daily source of inspiration. As I sit down to write about her, I find myself stalling—afraid I will not do her justice. I have known Cora for 18 years, virtually my entire career. She has been a constant force in my life, in the firmest yet gentlest of ways.

Before we met, I already knew her by reputation. She was "the formidable Cora Weiss," peace activist and convener extraordinaire. I finally met her in person in 1999, at a conference called the Hague Appeal for Peace, where Cora spearheaded the gathering of the world's leading visionaries, practitioners and artists to imagine a world without war. We launched dozens of initiatives—from networks warning against impending wars and alliances for eradicating small arms, to a global campaign aimed at bringing women's voices into the exclusive men's club of peace and security. Amidst the bustle of workshops, exhibits and people demanding her attention, Cora exuded authority, enthusiasm and incredible warmth. I was barely 30 years old, relatively new to the field of peacebuilding, and yet this world-renowned doyenne of peace activism treated me as an equal. She won my respect and trust immediately.

From then on, we worked together closely.

Through 1999 and 2000, Cora and I together with other colleagues worked intensively on mobilizing governments and Security Council support for what became the ground-breaking United Nations Security Council Resolution 1325 on Women, Peace and Security. We strategized and sparred, drafted and redrafted papers all in an effort to shift attitudes among Security Council members and get them to recognize the voices and experiences of women in war-torn settings and in peacemaking.

At the U.N. Cora knew everyone and everyone knew her, but she rolled up her sleeves and worked with us—a younger generation of women—to make things happen. She did not impose her views or her seniority. Quite the opposite: Cora welcomed fresh ideas and gave credit where it was due. These small acts may seem inconsequential, but they were profoundly significant. By supporting and encouraging us, Cora nurtured our confidence to think and act more boldly. From Cora I learned what it meant to lead by example, to truly practice what you preach. Perhaps most importantly she taught me that when the stakes are high, it takes us working together to collectively progress.

Our efforts succeeded. In October 2000 the U.N. Security Council adopted resolution 1325. We knew it was momentous but did not realize quite how historic and universal it would become. We had fought for the principle of women at the peace table because our colleagues from Sierra Leone to Sri Lanka were women building peace in the midst of wars. It was simply logical that these women should have a say in the future of their countries. Now, many years later, people still commend my commitment to this cause. But as Cora knows, when the cause is right—commitment and passion are inevitable.

Cora did not shy away from controversy. In 2008 we joined forces again to author a critique of the draft Security Council resolution 1820. The resolution was supposed to be an important next step after U.N. resolution 1325, but because it focused too heavily on women as rape victims and not enough on women as peacebuilders, we felt that it denigrated the spirit of 1325. "This agenda is about stopping and preventing all wars, not making them safe for women," said Cora.

Women's rights activists worldwide agreed with us, while one diplomat in New York admonished our lack of understanding of 1325. We chuckled at his ignorance and patronizing attitude, and demurely offered our assistance in redrafting the resolution. The draft text was sent to us promptly, and over the next 48 hours Cora and I provided real-time input. In the version we sent back, we reaffirmed the important role of women in peacemaking and referenced men and boys also as victims of sexual violence. (In the final text, we got mention of "civilians" because Libya, who sat on the Council, would not acknowledge men or boys as sexual violence victims.)

Through all of this work together, "the formidable Cora Weiss" gave way to Cora my fabulous friend, who got to know my family and traveled to Washington, D.C. in 2014 to speak at an awards ceremony on my behalf. And now, just as Cora did for me, I am trying to mentor a younger generation of peacewomen.

***

I met with Cora on a cold February day at her home in Manhattan to talk about who and what inspired her.

First, there was her mother, who volunteered for the Red Cross during World War II. "When young men came to the draft office to sign up, she'd bring them coffee and donuts and wish them well," recalls Cora. Her mother later ran the "Roosevelt for President" office in White Plains, New York—campaigning for a Democrat in a solidly Republican area. Cora's mother drove a car when women rarely drove, and returned to university to get a doctorate. In Cora's youth, U.S. First Lady Eleanor Roosevelt loomed large as a role model and later Cora was inspired by the anthropologist Ruth Benedict, a woman Cora says "believed in making the world safe for human differences."

As a college student in the 1950s, long before racial integration became a national issue, Cora ran a mixed-race swimming camp in Wisconsin. "I'd pick up the black kids from the other side of the tracks to join the white kids at camp." She wasn't trying to be radical, she says, it was simply common sense. "Everyone should learn how to swim, and these kids lived in a town with a gorgeous lake."

Soon after, Cora was volunteering for the "Joe Must Go" campaign aimed at recalling Wisconsin Senator Joseph McCarthy, who was leading a Cold War witch-hunt by accusing individual students, union leaders and other Americans of being Communists. Driving around Wisconsin, gathering signatures for the campaign, Cora was pelted with tomatoes, corn husks and potatoes. She learned an important lesson in organizing. "They pelted me because my car had New York plates," she noted. "If you organize at the grassroots, you have to be local— or at least have local plates!"

By the late 1950s, she was married to lawyer Peter Weiss, living in New York and volunteering at the U.N. African liberation movements aimed at freeing African countries from colonial power were inspiring to Cora and Peter, and Peter was a founding member of the American Committee on Africa. From Eduardo Mondlane—the first President of the Mozambican

Liberation Front—to South Africa's anti-apartheid politician Oliver Tambo—progressive African leaders appealing to the U.N. for independence found themselves at Cora's dinner table. Many became personal friends.

Kenyan trade unionist Tom Mboya arrived on Cora's doorstep with an ambitious goal during his 1959 speaking tour of American universities. Kenya was slated to gain its independence from Britain in 1963, but there were no Kenyan civil servants to run the country. Instead of asking for honoraria for his talks, Mboya asked universities for scholarships to send promising young Kenyans to the U.S. to study. Mboya's trip was a success, and hundreds of scholarships were promised to African students.

Cora and Peter helped to establish the African American Students Foundation—with Cora serving as the executive director—to raise more money to bring the Africans to study in the U.S. Celebrities Jackie Robinson (the first African American major league baseball player), Harry Belafonte (the famous African American artist, producer and activist) and Sidney Poitier (the African American Hollywood actor) helped fundraise, and the Joseph P. Kennedy Family Foundation was a major donor. In 1960, three planes were chartered, bringing the second large group of students from Africa to the U.S. It was a huge undertaking—and, at the time, a controversial one.

"We were pilloried by the elite organizations in international education and accused of lowering the standard of education because we were bringing in so many kids from 'the bush'," Cora recalls. But like all her other endeavours, Cora's efforts were a roaring success. Despite the ugliness of racism, Cora and her colleagues flew over 800 Kenyans to the U.S. in four years. To this day, says Cora, "When I go to Kenya, people say 'I slept on your living room floor'." As Mboya had hoped, most of the Kenyan students returned to civil service posts after independence. Among the Foundation's grantees were Wangari Maathai, the first female African Nobel peace laureate, and Barack Obama Sr., father of the 44th president of the United States.

As the 1960s rolled in, Cora also became immersed in the international Women Strike for Peace, protesting against atmospheric nuclear testing. "That's when I cut my political teeth," she says. "We learned we had to study the issues and become experts to be effective at mobilizing support." While she traveled abroad and marched for peace with Belgian Royals and British activists, her three young children stayed home. Cora packed her freezer with casseroles before every trip, and hired students to help care for her three kids.

A major turning-point in Cora's life came in the summer of 1969, when Cora met some North Vietnamese peace activist women who invited her to Hanoi. That fall, Cora co-chaired the mobilization for a huge anti-Vietnam war protest in Washington, D.C., and from there, traveled to Hanoi with two other women. She was determined to challenge U.S. President Richard M. Nixon's claim that the U.S. had to continue fighting because the Vietnamese were torturing U.S. prisoners of war (POWs). Cora helped form the Committee of Liaison with Servicemen Detained in North Vietnam whose members arranged to hand-deliver mail to downed American pilots, with the hope of determining who was still alive.

The action was a game-changer. Never before had civil society—driven by women—taken such action for peace. Cora drew media attention and criticism from powerful political forces. It embarrassed the Nixon administration, she says, that "a Jewish housewife from the Bronx could tell the government which of its soldiers were alive, when the government with all its might, could not."

A big break came in 1972. The Vietnamese wanted to release three POWs to the committee. Cora asked Bill Coffin, the Yale Divinity School Chaplain, international lawyer Richard Falk, and a young journalist, Peter Arnett, to join the delegation. From New York the group went to Bangkok and took the twice-a-week flight to Hanoi. Cora recalls that both sides to the conflict "stopped their surface to air missiles and bombings, until the plane landed." The POWs' release made headlines around the world.

Cora says her anti-Vietnam war experience offered important lessons. Peace activists have to mark their territory: being *for* peace does not mean supporting a warring party or government. Finding the human connections are important. Cora says for her work in Vietnam she learned a lot from Madame Nguyen Thi Binh, head of the North Vietnamese Women's Union. Finally, she says that peacemaking takes "dreaming of insanely creative things to do."

The 1980s took Cora back into the anti-nuclear movements and organizing with women on both sides of the Cold War. Cora approached Margarita Papandreou, the American wife of Greece's prime minister, for help in bringing together American and Russian women peace activists. Papandreou rented a boat so they could strategize on how to convince world leaders to stop the arms race. "American and Russian women stuck on a boat going around the Greek Islands! We finally negotiated and produced our joint statement," laughs Cora.

Cora's work convening women peacemakers during the Cold War foreshadowed our work on United Nations Security Council resolutions. Today our feminist networks are stronger and have broader reach across the globe, but I ask if she has regrets. She mentions a few, including not having focused more on teaching women to speak confidently in public and not recognizing sooner that "ovaries alone are not enough."

She notes that in the past her mantra was "women women everywhere and not enough in power." But in recent years Cora has grown cautious because so many women in politics are reactionary. The goal is not just to have women in power; they must also be women who have the courage to stand against war and fight for peace.

Cora's advice to future activists? "Take a holistic approach. The environment can't be cured without reducing military budgets. Inclusion and connecting issues is not dilettantism. It's seeing the world as a whole."

In peace work, preaching can overwhelm practice, but Cora is the exception. There is a common thread running through her life's work: doing what is right and necessary, regardless of whose feathers get ruffled. Invariably she has been on the right side and ahead of history, shaping the future. The evening beckons now, and I ask my friend one last question, "What drives you?" Cora doesn't hesitate. "Thinking about the world I want to leave for my children and grandchildren."

SANAM NARAGHI ANDERLINI is an Iranian-born British researcher and consultant to the United Nations on women, conflict and peacebuilding. She is co-founder and executive director of a non-governmental organization, International Civil Society Action Network. Along with Cora Weiss and other prominent women's rights advocates, she lobbied the U.N. Security Council to pass the historic UNSC Resolution 1325.

WANGARI MAATHAI

Wangari Maathai was a Kenyan environmental and political activist. In 1977, she founded the Green Belt Movement, an environmental non-governmental organization dedicated to the planting of trees, environmental conservation and women's rights. In 2004, she became the first African woman to be awarded the Nobel Peace Prize for her contributions to sustainable development, democracy and peace. In 2006, she helped to co-found the Nobel Women's Initiative. Wangari died in 2011.

SHOW UP, DO RIGHT, GIVE THANKS

By Alexandra Fuller

In November 2004, I went to Nairobi, Kenya to interview Wangari Maathai, who had recently been awarded the Nobel Peace Prize, making her the first African woman to win the prize. Among her many other accomplishments, Wangari had founded the Green Belt Movement, a social and environmental justice organization that protects and establishes forests, while at the same time giving the local communities where they grow—particularly the women living in their shelter—political, and therefore personal, power.

Wangari spent much of her life in opposition to the corrupt rule of Daniel arap Moi, second president of the republic of Kenya. But by the time I met her, Moi had been forced into retirement and Wangari was serving as assistant minister for environment and natural resources in the government of President Mwai Kibaki. She seemed unaffected by the sudden fame engendered by the Nobel prize, but was definitely amused by her countrymen's reaction which could be summed up as, "But all she did was make a noise and plant some trees!" Perhaps they were baffled because in east Africa, warmongering men generate many more headlines (think Uganda's Idi Amin or Ethiopia's Mengistu Haile Mariam) than do peace-fostering women.

In a culture that could be unforgivingly chauvinistic, stiflingly conformist and stymied by cronyism—Moi once famously dismissed Wangari as a madwoman, accusing her of having "insects in the head"—Wangari was refreshingly indefatigable, no-nonsense and irreverent. Excuses, laziness, and pompousness irritated her to no end. "Oh dear, take a shovel, dig a hole, put a tree in it!" she once told a group of expensively dressed men surrounding her at a tree-planting ceremony near the University of Kenya one bright hot afternoon during the time I was with her. "Or did you come to a tree-planting ceremony in a suit hoping to avoid the hard work?"

I fell in love with her on the spot.

In 2011, Wangari died of ovarian cancer. She was 71 years old. Her life, recounted in the 2006 autobiography *Unbowed*, was one of struggle, frequent disappointment and hard-won victories. I think it is easy for us to imagine that somewhere, in the back of her mind, she nursed an idea that one day she would be recognized for her good works, that the harassment and difficulties she experienced would be worth it in the end. But in truth, Wangari had no idea she would ever be recognized for her heroic efforts. In fact, it seemed far more likely she would be silenced forever by those she disturbed and angered within the Kenyan established elite.

"I don't really know why I care so much," she once said. "I just have something inside me that tells me that there is a problem, and I have got to do something about it. I think that is what I would call the God in me."

An Irreverent Power

In the years leading up to her becoming the first African woman to be awarded a Nobel prize, Wangari spoke out often and loudly against Daniel arap Moi's corrupt regime. More than once, Moi sent armed soldiers to beat, arrest and intimidate her. Once, she was beaten unconscious. On another occasion, soldiers besieged her home for three days.

Wangari loved justice and order. She craved a society in which civility, equal rights for women and an end to the violence of tribalism prevailed. But until that was the case, she was unafraid of the consequences of her frequent acts of civil disobedience. "When the government is bad, and you act for the good, it is you who will end up with the label," she told me. "Well, that is how it is. That's how it has always been."

An Optimism That Triumphed

"I wear yellow in defiance of global pessimism," Wangari once told me. Her government office in the middle of Nairobi was far from glamorous, but she hung pictures on the walls, and filled every available space with potted plants. Wherever she went, her goal was to make the space around her more alive, more viable, and more optimistic.

At the lowest point in her life—her husband had divorced her for being too outspoken and she had resigned from her job at the University of Nairobi to run for government office, only to be told she had missed the deadline to submit her name—Wangari consoled herself by planting trees.

"Well, I felt sorry for myself for a couple of hours," she told me. "And then I thought, 'This is not helping me, or the world.' So I got out of bed, I got dressed, and I went out to plant trees. You don't have to be in a good mood to plant a tree."

Fierceness Humbles

Wangari was an event. When she walked into a room, you couldn't help but stare. She spoke and you couldn't help but listen. But she didn't pander. "You put all that energy into smashing cars and setting fire to tires," she once scolded hundreds of students protesting water shortages on campus. "Did you think the drought was made just for you? You are students. Study the water cycle. Plant trees. When the rain comes, then you can demand water."

Wangari's talk had been scheduled for a stifling November day and the students had been waiting more than an hour to hear Wangari. Then when she did, her opening gambit was to rebuke her audience. I expected murmurings, disgruntlement. Instead, Wangari came to the end of her rebuke, flashed the students a big smile, and after a moment of stunned silence, there was a burst of spontaneous applause.

An Appetite for Simple

Wangari believed in simple solutions. She showed women how to grow vegetables in a sack outside their own back doors, and how to compost everything organic back into soil. She preferred eating foods harvested on the land she was standing on, in season. "We try to force these high-yielding non-native crops out of the soil at all times of the year, we exhaust the land, we use all the water, we grow fat. It takes almost no room to grow enough food to feed one family, and if you grow food that likes this soil and this climate, you are not fighting all the time."

I once asked Wangari how she had come to her credo of simplicity. "Is there any other philosophy?" she asked me back. Then she laughed, "If there is, it must have been invented by people with extra time on their hands." There was a beat. "Men," she said.

A Peace That Passes Ordinary Understanding

I can't think of Wangari without recalling how her strength seemed connected to a deeply personal faith. She was not blatantly religious—what I observed of her was that she was vigorously scientific and pragmatic—but it was hard to ignore her faith. It wasn't a submissive faith; Wangari's was a tough faith. It was a faith that had been tested, over and over, and found to be stalwart.

I asked Wangari how she had coped with her life, being separated from her three children while she sought work outside Kenya, ridiculed by her countrymen when her opposition to Moi was at its most contentious levels, losing her home and finding herself out of work more than once. But Wangari was sanguine. She said she always knew if she did just three things, everything would work out in the end:

Show up.

Do right.

Give thanks.

Because of Wangari

Wangari advocated her whole life for the rights of women, for the environment, and for social justice. By the time of her death, poor women in rural Kenya had planted 30 million trees. Wangari understood that women are always the first to suffer from environmental degradation because "they are the ones who walk for hours looking for water, who fetch firewood, who provide food for their family." She took a simple idea—planting trees—and made out of it something universal, sustainable and inspiring.

Doing great work doesn't need to be complicated. In fact, there is something very compelling about Wangari's solution to environmental and political injustice. It was so simple that it hardly seemed like a movement. "When I first started, it was really an innocent response to the needs of women in rural areas. When we started planting trees to meet their needs, there was nothing beyond that. I did not see all the issues that I have come to deal with."

I spent such a short time with her, but I think of Wangari often. In fact, WWWD or "What Would Wangari Do?" is a pretty good way for me to assess whether or not I am acting out of fear, or from what she would call the God within me. The one thing she made clear though was that the God within her, and the God within me, was the selfsame God. God just was able to do more with her as an instrument of peace than would seem possible.

ALEXANDRA FULLER is the award-winning author of five works of nonfiction including *Leaving Before the Rain Comes* and *Don't Let's Go to the Dogs Tonight,* a memoir about her childhood in conflict-torn Rhodesia (the country gained its independence and was later named Zimbabwe), Malawi and Zambia. She now lives in the U.S.

ELIZABETH BECKER

In 1973, as a correspondent for *The Washington Post,* Elizabeth Becker became one of the first Western journalists to extensively report on the civil war in Cambodia and the rise of the Khmer Rouge. Now an award-winning journalist and author, she has written a number of books, including *When the War Was Over: Cambodia and the Khmer Rouge Revolution.*

DOCUMENTING GENOCIDE

By Bopha Phorn

I grew up in the 1980s in Cambodia's Prey Veng province, a remote agricultural region far from the country's capital of Phnom Penh. I was born in a decade that followed one of the worst periods in my country's history: the civil war and subsequent uprising of the Khmer Rouge regime, which led to the brutal death of a quarter of my country's population. I was an avid reader and writer from an early age. I had minimal access to newspapers, but I read all the news I could get my hands on. I gleaned pieces of my country's recent dark past through my reading, and became fascinated by the journalists behind the stories. By the time I was 10, I knew I wanted to be a journalist.

This was not easy for my family to accept, as I was one of two girls among six siblings in a relatively traditional Cambodian family, where it was the girl's job to help with household chores and the family business. I had to work hard to convince my family to allow me to attend school and study, as they felt there was plenty "more useful" work for me to do at home. After I completed high school, my family pushed me to end my studies. But I was determined to become a journalist. I knew I needed to attend university in order to achieve my dream job, so with financial support from my sister, I started a money lending business. It was a risky gig, but it allowed me to gain the financial independence I needed to complete my university education.

I don't know exactly what inspired me to become a journalist, especially since it meant fighting the conventions of my culture. I do know, however, that I found a role model along the way whose life and work inspired me to continue to pursue my dream despite the barriers I faced.

I discovered Elizabeth Becker while I was working at the *Cambodia Daily*, decades after she had first covered Cambodia. An American, Becker came to Cambodia in 1972, directly after completing graduate studies in South Asian politics. The country was plunging into a gruesome civil war, and she soon became a war correspondent for the *Washington Post*.

I learned a lot about the worst period in my country from Becker, and I came to see her as someone whose example I could follow, partly because she had chosen to work in war-torn Cambodia when she could have pursued a more comfortable career path.

Becker reflected on her experience reporting in the country in a 2015 *Washington Post* article.

> *At that time Cambodia was in the middle of a brutal civil war, triggered by the neighboring struggle in Vietnam. The United States was underwriting the corrupt government; communist Vietnam was supporting the Khmer Rouge.*
>
> *For two years, I reported on a country being rapidly disfigured by warfare and a massive American bombing campaign. I watched as the once-elegant capital came apart, with barbed wire snaking in front of cafes and neighborhoods overcrowded with families fleeing the countryside.*

When I finally landed a job as a journalist, I was very happy to see posters of Elizabeth Becker stuck on the wall of my office. The images helped me to persist with this career and stay resilient when it was at its most dangerous or demoralizing. Even today, in a much more stable environment than when Becker worked here, Cambodia is not a particularly friendly place for journalists. Censorship is common, media reports that don't reflect well on the government are discouraged, and the threat of violence is always present. On one occasion I received such serious threats from high-level government officials for my coverage of Cambodia's drug trade that I needed to vacate my home for a while.

Needless to say, it takes resolve to stay in this career in my country; certain things have helped me keep mine. One is a book a colleague recommended after I'd first started working as a journalist. It tells the story of the Khmer Rouge and how they fought against French colonial rule, overthrew the Cambodian government and then turned Cambodia into a horrific authoritarian state. Infamous Khmer Rouge leader Pol Pot re-constructed Cambodia by forcing millions of people from cities to work on communal farms in the countryside, eliminating intellectuals and other citizens deemed detrimental to his vision.

When I was partway through reading this book, I realized it was written by my idol, Elizabeth Becker. The book is called *When the War Was Over*, and I keep it close as a reminder of the kind of journalist I'm striving to become. It is not only a well-researched account of the complex politics of the time, but Becker also places a very human story at its centre—that of Hout Bophana. While conducting research for the book in Cambodia in 1981, Becker discovered love letters between Bophana and her husband, Ly Sitha, in an official dossier at Tuol Sleng, the once secret Khmer Rouge prison. The letters, and Becker's account of them, reveal a tragic love story: a couple separated while fleeing the civil war. Each presumed the other one dead, but Bophana had escaped to a provincial city, where she was raped by a Cambodian soldier, became pregnant and gave birth to a son. Ly Sitha had escaped to a monastery to avoid being drafted into the war.

The pair found each other years later, having been forced through circumstances they could not control into opposite ends of the hierarchy of Khmer Rouge rule—Ly, a fighter with the Khmer Rouge and Bophana, an educated and defiant citizen of the regime they had defeated. Circumstances kept the couple apart, but they continued writing to each other, plotting plans to escape and be together. Ultimately, Bophana and Ly Sitha were separately captured, tortured and murdered because of their letters.

In *When the War Was Over*, Becker explains why Bophana's profound love was dangerous to the regime:

> [T]he Khmer Rouge were threatened by all expressions of love — between husband and wife, parents and children, friends and colleagues. Everyone had to renounce personal intimacies … By writing to each other, {Sitha} and Bophana had refused to live a solitary, isolated and emotionally barren life. That was perhaps Bophana's greatest crime.

The Tuol Sleng prison is now a museum in Phnom Penh. Twice-daily, the museum shows a movie based on Bophana's story; she has become a symbol of the Cambodian lives destroyed through complex geo-political and ideological battles outside of their control. Cambodians know the story of Bophana, and all that it symbolizes, because of Elizabeth Becker.

I am also inspired by Becker's choice to regularly return to Cambodia. She left the country in 1974, disillusioned by all the destruction that she'd witnessed as a war correspondent, expecting it to get much worse (which it did), and planning to move on with her career. Over the next few years, however, she heard disturbing stories about the Khmer Rouge and of forced evacuations and executions. The news was scarce because the regime had cut off links to the outside world. I think the lack of information coming out of the country may have spurred Becker's determination to return: she may have feared the gruesome truth would escape the rest of the world's notice if she didn't go investigate and report on it herself.

It took several years and much negotiation, but in 1978 she secured a journalism visa. In a 2015 article for the *Washington Post* Becker writes: "Carrying one of the only two journalist visas ever issued by the {Khmer Rouge} regime, I spent two weeks under heavy surveillance, investigating the stories I'd heard from refugees about vast labor camps, torture chambers and summary executions."

Becker's entire visit was controlled and there was very little freedom for her to conduct any investigations. On the last day of her visit she was granted a rare interview with Pol Pot. She describes her time with him as a one-way lecture during which she was not permitted to speak, but through which she came to understand the depths of his fanaticism and charisma, and how the country had descended so deeply into an otherwise inexplicable horror.

Later that same night, a gun-wielding attacker entered the guesthouse where she and her colleagues were staying. "We were assaulted just hours before we were scheduled to leave," she wrote. "When a Cambodian official finally rescued me, I learned that my colleague, the academic Malcolm Caldwell, had been killed, shot several times at point-blank range… Though I can't prove it, I believe that someone in the government had opposed our trip and wanted to silence us."

Losing a colleague and barely escaping with her life must have been very traumatic for Becker. But it didn't stop her: she came back to Cambodia several times over the next six years to conduct research for *When the War Was Over.*

Then, decades later, she returned to Cambodia to testify at a Cambodian court created under an agreement between the Cambodian government and the United Nations. With the purpose of bringing justice to Cambodians and promoting national reconciliation, the court was formally established in 2006 and brings to trial senior leaders and those considered most responsible for crimes of starvation, torture, execution and forced labour committed during the time of the Khmer Rouge.

Of the prosecution's request for her to testify, Becker explains in her 2015 *Washington Post* article:

> *I was the only Western journalist to witness both the devastating Cambodian civil war and the Khmer Rouge regime that followed. I had exclusive interviews with top officials, who'd confessed to the use of torture chambers and forced labor under hideous conditions. I had researched dozens of Cambodians who'd been arrested, tortured and killed.*

It is a difficult decision for a journalist to participate as a witness. In the same article, Becker writes of the dilemma: "If dictators and war criminals knew that reporters might testify against them in court, would it make attacks like the one I experienced more common?" She ultimately decided she needed to participate. "With Bophana on my mind, I agreed to testify. I had been privileged, as a journalist, to collect materials and experiences that no one else had. With that came responsibility. I also wanted to honor the systems of law that are slowly bringing justice to countries like Cambodia."

Becker was invited by the prosecution to appear as an expert in the trial of two of the regime's most senior survivors: Pol Pot's deputy, Nuon Chea, and Khieu Samphan, the former head of state, both charged with genocide, grave breaches of the 1949

Geneva Conventions, and crimes against humanity. Their case was divided into two components, the first of which ended in August 2014 with their conviction for crimes against humanity and sentences of life in prison, which they have subsequently appealed. Becker's appearance is linked to the second part of the case. In February 2015, she took to the stand, an experience she describes as difficult and overwhelmingly emotional at times.

"Each day, seven people brutalized by the regime were given seats in the courtroom. Whenever I felt overwhelmed, I was reassured looking at their faces, knowing they had petitioned the court to bring justice."

Becker's ongoing bravery speaks to me on a profoundly personal level. In 2012, I was investigating claims of illegal logging and environmental exploitation in a protected area of Cambodia with another journalist, Olesia Plokhii, and an environmental activist, Chut Wutty, when gunmen began firing at our vehicle with AK-47s. Chut was shot, and we tried unsuccessfully to save him. I still do not have enough strength to go back to the province where the incident occurred. Becker has faced worse situations in my country and is still willing to come back to pursue the truth and work for justice here.

I am so passionate about being a journalist that I feel if I had to stop, I would stop breathing. So I make myself a bit blind to the dangers, and also deaf to the challenges of being a female reporter in a place where colleagues and government officials regularly ask me about my age and my marital status. Thanks to the example of Elizabeth Becker and other brave journalists, I am keeping my dream of being a journalist alive, and aspire to become the kind of person of whom she would be proud.

BOPHA PHORN is a Cambodian independent journalist who has reported for the *The Cambodia Daily* and other publications. In 2013, she won the International Women's Media Foundation's Courage in Journalism Award for her work investigating claims of illegal logging in a protected area of the Cambodian jungle.

GLORIA STEINEM

Gloria Steinem is one of the most influential and defining feminists of the past century. Born in the U.S., Steinem started as a journalist and came to prominence as a leader of the women's movement in the 1960s. Now in her 80s, Steinem continues to write about and speak on issues impacting women around the world, including peace and security.

TOWARD A FEMINIST FOREIGN POLICY

by Valerie M. Hudson

Gloria Steinem's name has become synonymous with feminism, but it's also true to say her life has been devoted to the cause of peace. In her 81st year, Steinem joined a group of 30 women peacemakers who marched (or attempted to march) across the Demilitarized Zone (DMZ) separating the two Koreas, to highlight the political-military stalemate there. Two Nobel laureates, Mairead Maguire and Leymah Gbowee, also marched. This was no orchestrated photo op. Steinem explained that they'd arrived not knowing if they'd actually be allowed to cross or not, and that it was "remarkable" that they were given permission to do so by the two opposed governments. "North and South Korean women can't walk across the DMZ legally," she said. "We from other countries can. So I feel we are walking on their behalf."

To dare to envision peace is a profoundly subversive act, and always has been. While Steinem has contributed toward the building of a more peaceful world in many ways, such as the DMZ walk, one of her foremost contributions has been to envision, articulate, and help realize a world where the global war against women has an end.

Ending the war against women is not some add-on or tangent to the cause of peace between races, peoples, and nations— it is the precondition for such peace. There cannot be peace between nations until there is peace between the two halves of humanity, the mothers and fathers of all living and all yet to live. This understanding is the great gift Steinem has given to three generations of humankind now—a gift we will pass on to our own daughters and sons.

Steinem sees a connection between what we have chosen to normalize in male-female relations, and what we see at the level of state and society. "The family is the basic cell of the government," she explains, "it is where we are trained to believe that we are human beings or that we are chattel, it is where we are trained to see the sex and race divisions and become callous to injustice even if it is done to ourselves, to accept as biological a full system of authoritarian government."

Truly, then, we should not be surprised that societies rooted in male dominance over females are not peaceful or democratic; as Steinem notes, "We're never going to have democratic countries or peaceful countries until we have democratic or peaceful families." Why? Because you must teach men to dominate in order to maintain a male-dominated system. And that is a very ugly education, indeed, where the first to be dominated are those within men's own families who are different from them: women. Domestic violence is the seedbed of all other violence based on difference. "This is the first form of violence, domination, power we see as children," explains Steinem. "It normalizes every other form."

This education in domination not only harms women—it harms men as well. Steinem says that when she talks to groups of men they often bring up how masculine roles have limited them, and how they missed having real, present loving fathers, as their dads were always trying to fit an ideal of masculinity, which did not include that. Because men have been taught that they have to "prove" their masculinity in a way women do not, and because masculinity has been constructed upon notions of domination and control, men's lives can easily become inhumane. It's a life that brings no lasting happiness. In a way, then, feminism is humanism, for it seeks to liberate both men and women from destructively contorted sex roles.

Steinem maintains that women will tend to be much better peacemakers until the masculine role is humanized. Women are integral to peacebuilding, for they have not been sidelined by the need to prove their sex role through conflict and aggression. Steinem points out that people thought achieving peace in Ireland and in Liberia would be impossible, but in both countries women from both sides started working together and did the impossible—achieved peace.

If peace cannot be built without women then one of the most important steps that could be taken to ensure a more peaceful world would be empowering women globally:

> *The worldwide reduction of violence against females should be a core goal of our foreign policy. It should be, given its outcome, its demonstrable outcome in every major country in the world ... Instead, what happens is the "it would be nice" principle—"It would be nice if women were more equal in Afghanistan, but it's not important." And many of our officials have said specifically that women's rights have nothing to do with nationalism, peace conferences, peace processes, all kinds of things. We could, for instance, actually put some teeth into UNSCR 1325 ... We have the principle, but it is on paper only, it is not enacted.*

In an interview I did with Steinem in 2013, she opened my eyes to just how vastly different our foreign policy would be if we took the cause of women seriously. She recounted an incident that happened just after the Soviet invasion of Afghanistan in 1979. She attended a briefing of women's organizations in a State Department auditorium toward the end of President Jimmy Carter's tenure. Although the subject was an upcoming U.N. women's conference and Afghanistan wasn't mentioned, the Soviets had rolled into Kabul that very day. Newspapers were full of articles about the mujahideen—the Islamist guerrilla fighters in Afghanistan—and their declaration of war against their own Soviet-supported government. Their leaders gave three reasons for why they wanted to drive the Soviets out: girls were permitted to go to school; girls and women could no longer be married off without their consent; and women were being invited to political meetings.

During the discussion that followed the meeting, Steinem stood up and posed an obvious question to her State Department hosts: Given what the mujahideen themselves had said that day, wasn't the United States supporting the wrong side? Steinem remembers the question falling into that particular hush reserved for the ridiculous. She doesn't remember the exact answer, but the State Department made it clear the United States opposed anything the Soviets supported—the government spokesman made no mention that the United States was arming violent, antidemocratic, misogynist religious extremists.

It was clear that matters of war and peace were about realpolitik and oil pipelines—and not about honoring the human rights of the more peaceful female half of the human race. And so it happened that the mujahideen waged their brutal war with weapons supplied by the United States and, of course, Saudi Arabia—the birthplace of the doctrinaire interpretation of Islam known as Wahhabism. Together, they gave birth to the Taliban, al-Qaeda, and other affiliated terror networks that now reach far beyond the borders of Afghanistan. Steinem says she has never stopped regretting that she didn't chain herself to the seats of that State Department auditorium in public protest.

Feminism, then, when you look at it as Steinem does, as the recognition of the full humanity and full equality of both men and women, *is* peace work. When U.S. President Barack Obama presented Steinem with the Presidential Medal of Freedom in 2013 for her work advancing women's rights and civil rights, she made the connection between the two explicit by saying the medal meant so much because it was, in a way, for waging peace. She explained that the gender division, in which there is a subject and an object, a masculine and feminine, a dominant and passive, is what normalizes other violence that has to do with race and class and ethnicity and sexuality. Men's idea that they must defeat each other in order to be masculine, she explained, "is the root of the false idea that we are ranked as human beings rather than linked."

Steinem argues there is a better vision—an embrace of difference without hierarchy. When we encounter that first difference between male and female, a profound choice is placed before us: we can rank those who are different, or we can link them. Steinem urges us to choose the latter: "Difference is the source of learning ... Difference is a gift, so that we understand and don't fear ... We live in a world of 'either/or.' We're trying to make a world of 'and.' So it is about shared humanity in perfect balance with difference."

Steinem once described herself as a "hope-aholic," which seems like a very good way to describe peacemakers. It is a life filled with incorrigible aspiration for a better world, and the tenacity to work for its realization. Part of this hope is that one day the vision you see will seem obvious to everyone: "I think that being a feminist means that you see the world whole instead of half. It shouldn't need a name, and one day it won't."

And as for Steinem herself? "I hope to live to 100. There is so much to do."

VALERIE M. HUDSON is a professor and award-winning author who was named one of the Top 100 Global Thinkers by *Foreign Policy* in 2009. She has written or co-authored a number of books focused on gender and foreign policy including *Sex and World Peace* (2012), which outlines how the security of women is a key factor in the security and peace of the state. She is the founder of The WomanStats Project, which seeks to develop the most comprehensive database on the situation and status of women throughout the world. Most recently, she is the co-author of *The Hillary Doctrine: Sex and American Foreign Policy.*

BETTY OYELLA BIGOMBE

Betty Oyella Bigombe was a key figure in peace negotiations with the Lord's Resistance Army in Uganda starting in the 1990s, acting as the main mediator between the LRA and the Ugandan government, even holding talks with rebel leader Joseph Kony. She is now the Senior Director for Fragility, Conflict and Violence at the World Bank.

THE STRENGTH OF "SOFT" POWER

By Doreen Baingana

I have tried to imagine a woman in a crowded vehicle, slowly making its way through thick bush. She is the lone female in a group of village elders and religious leaders. They have left the nearest town, Gulu, in northern Uganda, miles behind, passed scattered hut-filled villages, and now it is just the sound of their car swishing through the long elephant grass, bird-calls, the relentless dry sun of the savannah, and their own fearful thoughts that fill the air. The woman is Betty Oyella Bigombe, and she has persuaded these men to join her in meeting one of the most murderous men in recent history, rebel leader Joseph Kony. They hope to persuade him to talk peace with the Ugandan government. Why on earth would she do this?

Women who choose to engage in the predominantly male arena of war fascinate me. It was recent interest in another woman who played a major role in Uganda's war-torn history that led me to Betty Bigombe. For the past two years I have been writing a novel about Alice Lakwena, a female rebel leader who fought against the government in 1987-88. She believed she'd been anointed by the Holy Spirit to lead a holy war to cleanse Uganda of evil and initiate a just rule. She was defeated, but remnants of her army joined a young man named Joseph Kony, who was from the same Acholi ethnic group and formed the now-notorious Lord's Resistance Army (LRA). He too claimed to be on a holy mission to overthrow the government and rule Uganda according to the Ten Commandments. Betty Bigombe made two major attempts to end this guerrilla war by bringing two opposing sides to the negotiating table.

It is bitterly ironic that Kony's methods have been the exact opposite of the Ten Commandments. His group is notorious for raiding and burning villages, murdering tens of thousands of civilians, displacing about two million people, and kidnapping and forcefully recruiting as many as 20,000 children. Many of the captured girls were forced to become sex slaves. The terror caused by Kony and the LRA led the government to herd the mostly Acholi population away from their homes into camps, supposedly for their own safety. Civil war ravaged much of northern Uganda for about 20 years.

I see two powerful Acholi women standing like bookends on either side of the evil Kony period in Uganda's history. Alice Lakwena truly believed that peace could come through a "righteous" war. Betty Bigombe believes the opposite: that peace is best achieved by peaceful means, and most especially through dialogue.

Bigombe started her peace work long before Kony's brutality reached its apex. In 1988, President Yoweri Museveni appointed her as minister of state for the North to represent him in peace efforts. She was working on development projects across Africa at the time, and refused the position at first. The president had selected Bigombe because she was one of the few influential Acholi who supported his new government. The brutal way Museveni's army tried to quell rebellion in the North had caused widespread tension and distrust. After assessing damage done by government forces in the East and North, Bigombe finally agreed to take on the job of peacebuilder.

Right from the start, there was resistance to her efforts from all sides. Army officers preferred fighting the rebels to engaging in dialogue, not the least because they allegedly benefitted financially from the resources that fuelled civil war. The rebels claimed that by appointing "just a girl" to initiate peace efforts, the government had proven they were not serious about reaching a settlement. Bigombe was also called a traitor because, even though she was Acholi, who are from the North, she was now working for a "southern" government.

None of this deterred Bigombe. What inspires and fascinates me most is that she used methods perceived as being "feminine," and therefore somehow as less effective, to successfully get the warring sides to sit down together—in itself a major feat.

Bigombe took time to gain the trust of all sides. She consulted extensively in Internally Displaced People's camps, listening to the war stories of local people and even buying them food and liquor—to "loosen their tongues and open their minds," as she says. She also danced with them around the communal fire every evening, as is customary, and encouraged them to criticize leaders so that she could carry their concerns and messages to a higher level.

Eventually, however, Bigombe headed deep into the bush with six religious leaders, all of them deeply fearful, to meet with Kony and his mostly teenaged and often drug-dependent soldiers. Both sides talked far into the night. After six similar encounters, with Kony now referring to her as "Mummy Bigombe," and two years of tireless work in 1992-94, she actually persuaded the rebels and government representatives to agree to a peace deal. Critics who said Bigombe was not tough enough or did not have enough authority to broker peace—none too subtle attacks based on her womanhood—were put to shame. "Soft power" had gotten the two sides to the negotiating table for the very first time.

To Bigombe's bitter disappointment, President Museveni, advised by his army officials, called off peace talks just two weeks before the agreement was due to be signed. Even so, her efforts were not wasted, because attacks and atrocities ceased while the peace process was moving forward, saving an untold number of lives. It was no wonder the government named Bigombe "Ugandan Woman of the Year" in 1994.

Betty Bigombe left Uganda to do a Masters in public administration at Harvard, and later got a job at the World Bank. But her heart remained at home. Ten years later, from the comfort of her house in suburban Maryland, she saw her own face on TV. It was a television news piece about an attack by Kony's army on a village in northeastern Uganda, called Barlonya, where more than 200 people had been massacred. The newscaster said only one person had managed to persuade Kony's army to talk peace 10 years before: Betty Bigombe. After seeing that story, Bigombe decided to leave her World Bank job and her two children in the U.S., and return to Uganda to give peace another try. This time, however, she would have to rely on her own resources because she was not a government representative.

I ask myself whether, in Bigombe's shoes, I would have made the same decision. I happen to have attended the same high school she did, Gayaza High School in Kampala—the first girls' boarding high school in Uganda—though many years later. I mention this not only because I am proud of this slight connection, but also because she absolutely exemplifies our school motto: "Never give up." While for many of us it is merely a feel-good slogan, Betty Bigombe has lived these words through and through. Instead of shrugging her shoulders at yet another terrible news item, as most of us do, she packed her bags and changed countries to try and do something about it—all over again.

Like many Ugandans, I am almost inured to conflict, provided it does not directly affect me and mine. I am not proud to admit this. I have lived through Idi Amin's reign of terror, through the chaotic changes in leadership that followed, through Museveni's five-year "bush war" and his coup d'état in 1986, then his 30 years in power (although I spent some of those years outside Uganda), which included the 20-year rebel war in the North. Many of us have survived this turmoil by detaching from politics and focusing on our personal lives, keeping things as normal as possible while we study, work and raise our children. And, in fact, we largely succeed in creating happy, fulfilling lives right here, despite headline news. But there are a few special people like Betty Bigombe, who simply cannot step around public tragedy, who feel compelled to try and end it.

Bigombe probably could not bring herself to imagine that her move would mean two years away from her family. Based mostly in a hotel in Gulu, she tried once again to bring the two warring sides to negotiate. She spent a lot of time on the phone: coaxing, encouraging, scolding and doing a lot of patient listening to all sides. In some instances she even used her considerable charm to convince army officers to hold off renewing attacks.

A journalist once reported going with her to a meeting with rebels. When they arrived at the remote bush location, they were immediately surrounded by young boys—barely in their teens but heavily armed, with their fingers on the triggers. Bigombe offered a sack of rice, which they eyed with wary hunger. They didn't take it, but the door of trust had been nudged open. The rebels kept asking her for supplies and she sent what she could, using her own money, with some assistance from aid groups. Critics said she was being manipulated, but she knew that if the rebels had the basics, they would have less need to raid and ransack villages. This practical, down-to-earth thinking not only saved lives but also led the parties to trust in and feel goodwill toward her and her efforts.

Bigombe has said that at times, silence was the most effective weapon in her arsenal. She recalls one phone conversation with President Museveni when he expressed complete impatience with rebel demands, which included complete military withdrawal by the army from northern Uganda. He talked on and on down the line, but Bigombe did not answer. She simply let him talk and when he paused, she didn't say a word. It was her silence that finally cut through his anger, her silence that spoke volumes, saying, in effect: "Do you really want to blow it all up or do you want to move toward peace?"

Bigombe's brave and selfless work led to a halt in the atrocities. The number of children being kidnapped decreased dramatically since 2004. Her efforts laid the groundwork for the "Juba Talks" between the Museveni government and a Lord's Resistance Army delegation in 2007, which led to a major, if temporary, ceasefire. The LRA were eventually chased out of Uganda, but they still carry out scattered attacks in remote regions of the Central African Republic and the Democratic Republic of the Congo.

Betty Bigombe returned to her children in the U.S., and still works for peace as the Senior Director of Fragility, Conflict and Violence at the World Bank. To her strengths as a researcher and policy maker, she also brings immense skills as a practitioner who has been in the trenches and gotten her hands dirty. My hope is that her so-called soft power methods will no longer be viewed as unorthodox but could become central to peace efforts everywhere. My other hope is that by writing about women in war, such as Betty Bigombe, I am contributing, in my own unorthodox way, to peace.

DOREEN BAINGANA is an award-winning author and editor from Uganda. Her short-story collection, *Tropical Fish*, won the Commonwealth Prize First Book Award in 2006.

HELEN CALDICOTT

Helen Caldicott is an Australian physician and one of the world's leading anti-nuclear advocates. She is an internationally renowned speaker and author on the subject of the nuclear age's hazards to human and environmental health, and is the president of The Helen Caldicott Foundation, which aims to raise awareness about the dangers of nuclear power and promote a nuclear energy and weapons-free world.

INSPIRATION FOR THE FIRST NUKE-FREE COUNTRY

By Marilyn Waring

If you were growing up in New Zealand and Australia post World War II, there's a chance you knew about the United States using the Marshall Islands as a nuclear testing site from 1947 until 1962. In an agreement signed with the United Nations, the U.S. government held the Marshall Islands as a "trust territory" and detonated nuclear devices in this pristine area of the Pacific Ocean—leading, in some instances, to huge levels of radiation fall-out, health effects, and the permanent displacement of many island people. In all, the U.S. government conducted 105 underwater and atmospheric tests. You would have also known that the British conducted seven atmospheric tests between 1956 and 1963 on traditional Aboriginal land, in Maralinga, Australia.

It may be that you read Neville Shute's 1957 novel *On the Beach,* in which people in Melbourne, Australia wait for deadly radiation to spread from a Northern Hemisphere nuclear war. This book made a memorable impact on Helen when she read it as a teenager. When I was a teenager, some years later, I read Bertrand Russell's 1959 classic, *Common Sense and Nuclear Warfare.*

Both Helen and I saw Peter Watkin's *The War Game*, a BBC documentary drama about nuclear war and the consequences in an English city. In New Zealand the film was restricted for children unless accompanied by an adult, so I had to get my father to take me. *The War Game* won the Oscar for the best documentary in 1965.

France began its series of over 175 nuclear tests at Mururoa, in the South Pacific, in 1966. At least 140 of these tests were above ground. In 1973, the New Zealand and Australian governments took France to the World Court for continued atmospheric testing, and forced the last tests underground. The testing finally came to an end in 1976.

In New Zealand the U.S. Navy made regular visits between 1976 and 1983 with nuclear-powered and, most likely, nuclear-armed, ships. These visits produced spectacular protest fleets in the Auckland and Wellington harbours, when hundreds of New Zealanders—in yachts of all sizes, in motor boats and canoes, even on surf boards—surrounded the vessels and tried to bring them to a complete stop. By 1978, a campaign began in New Zealand to declare borough and city council areas nuclear-free and, by the early 1980s, this symbolic movement had quickly gained momentum, covering more than two-thirds of the New Zealand population.

Helen Caldicott and I had not met up to this point, but these were shared parts of our history and consciousness when Helen visited New Zealand in 1983.

***

Helen Caldicott graduated with a medical degree from University of Adelaide Medical School in 1961. She moved to the United States, becoming an Instructor in paediatrics at Harvard Medical School and was on the staff of the Children's Hospital Medical Centre in Boston, Massachusetts. In the late 1970s, Helen became the President of Physicians for Social Responsibility. This group was founded when Helen was finishing medical school, quickly making its mark by documenting the presence of Strontium-90, a highly radioactive waste product of atmospheric nuclear testing, in children's teeth. The landmark finding eventually led to the Limited Nuclear Test Ban treaty, which ended atmospheric nuclear testing.

But it was the Three Mile Island accident that changed Helen's life. An equipment failure resulted in a loss of cooling water to the core of a reactor at the Three Mile Island Nuclear Generating Station in Pennsylvania, causing a partial meltdown. Operator failure meant that 700,000 gallons of radioactive cooling water ended up in the basement of the reactor building. It was the most serious nuclear accident to that date in the U.S. Helen published *Nuclear Madness* the same year. In it she wrote: "As a physician, I contend that nuclear technology threatens life on our planet with extinction. If present trends continue, the air we breathe, the food we eat, and the water we drink will soon be contaminated with enough radioactive pollutants to pose a potential health hazard far greater than any plague humanity has ever experienced." In 1980, Helen resigned from her paid work positions to work full time on the prevention of nuclear war.

In 1982, Canadian director Terre Nash filmed a lecture given by Helen Caldicott to a New York state student audience. Nash's consequent National Film Board of Canada documentary *If You Love this Planet* was released during the term of U.S. President Ronald Reagan, at the height of Cold War nuclear tensions between the United States and the Soviet Union. The U.S. Department of Justice moved quickly to designate the film "foreign propaganda," bringing a great deal of attention to the film. It went on to win the 1982 Academy Award for Documentary Short Subject. That same year, Helen addressed about 750,000 people in Central Park, New York in the biggest anti-nuke rally in the United States to that date.

In 1983, I was serving as a member of the New Zealand parliament, having been elected eight years earlier at the age of 23. Our parliament established a Disarmament and Arms Control Select Committee to conduct hearings on the possibility of making New Zealand a nuclear-free zone. During this critically important time, Helen was invited to New Zealand on a lecture tour. The documentary *If You Love This Planet* was shown at her speaking engagements.

I did not get to meet her, nor hear any of her lectures in person, as I was working in parliament every night. But I did follow the media coverage.

Helen told the magazine the *Listener* about having observed five-star generals in U.S. congressional and senate committees complaining that the Russian missiles were bigger than the American ones. "The Russian missiles are very big (and) inaccurate and clumsy. America has very small, very accurate missiles, which are better at killing people and destroying targets," she explained. A frequent message in her talks to New Zealand audiences was the redundant overkill capacity of both superpowers. Caldicott noted to her audiences that "[T]he U.S. has 30,000 bombs and Russia 20,000."

I had sat in a New Zealand parliamentary committee hearing some months earlier, when a government colleague, brandishing a centrefold of a Russian submarine, excitedly called for us to "Look at how big it is." I had thought that no one would believe me if I had repeated such an inane banality—when an adult male was more impressed by the size of the submarine than its capacity to destroy life on this planet.

Helen's public addresses were grounded in the potential impact of nuclear weapons. "Imagine a 20-megaton bomb targeted on Auckland," she told audiences in New Zealand. "The explosion, five times the collective energy of all the bombs dropped in the Second World War, digs a hole three-quarters of a mile wide by 800 feet deep and turns people, buildings and dirt into radioactive dust. Everyone up to six miles will be vaporised, and up to 20 miles they will be dead or lethally injured. People will be instantly blinded looking at the blast within 40 miles. Many will be asphyxiated in the fire storm."

Helen did not hold back, explaining that nuclear war means "blindness, burning, starvation, disease, lacerations, haemorrhaging, millions of corpses and an epidemic of disease." Helen's dramatic and blunt style reduced many in her audiences to tears. She always ended her talks with a call to action—especially to parents—as she strongly believes that nuclear disarmament is "the ultimate medical and parenting issue of our time."

To those who would claim New Zealand was not a target she had a short reply: "Trident submarines in ports are targeted. They are a first strike target. It is much easier to destroy subs when they are in dock than it is when they are submerged in the ocean."

In 2015, I asked Helen how she managed to deliver such bad news and yet keep her audiences with her. "Being a doctor helps because you have to learn to negotiate with a patient and with language they can understand," she explained. "You have to convert the medical diagnosis and treatment to lay language. I also have to keep them awake sometimes by letting them laugh because it relieves their tension and because the stuff I say is pretty awful." Helen told me that she practices "global preventative medicine."

Helen's tour through New Zealand in 1983 had a huge, and lasting, impact. At one stop, Helen addressed over 2,000 people at a public event in Auckland. The librarian with whom I corresponded looking for old newspaper reports of Helen's visit, wrote to me: "Her chillingly detailed description of the effects of a nuclear device detonated over the hall in which we were sitting remains rooted in my psyche to this day! ...The other message I most recall is the dichotomy she evoked between the destructive drive of 'old men' rulers, the instigators of war, versus the procreative energy of mothers most impelled to oppose them—which, however reductive, retains the compelling logic of a truism!"

Helen's approach was transformative in New Zealand. Helen's speaking events packed auditoriums, and overflows of audiences had to be accommodated using loud speaker systems. People responded strongly to this woman, whose life work involved caring for children, speaking about medical effects of fallout, and speaking without the use of the clichéd military and defence ideological rhetoric that treated people as if they were simpletons who couldn't understand. Her speeches inspired people to act. After Helen spoke, the volume of mail delivered to my parliamentary office increased—particularly from women.

On May 24, 1983, 20,000 women wearing white flowers and armbands and holding banners with peace signs marched quietly up a main street in Auckland to hold a huge rally and call for New Zealand to be nuke-free. It was one of the largest women's demonstrations in New Zealand's history. In her book, *Peace, Power and Politics – How New Zealand Became Nuclear Free*, Maire Leadbetter writes: "I am one of many activists who think of Helen Caldicott's visit as the point when the peace movement began to grow exponentially... Helen had a magical ability to motivate previously passive citizens to become activists."

Shortly after Helen's visit to New Zealand, in 1984, I advised that I intended to vote for the opposition-sponsored nuclear-free New Zealand legislation. This prompted conservative Prime Minister Rob Muldoon to call a snap election. Muldoon told media that my "feminist anti-nuclear stance" threatened his ability to govern.

The new Labour Government of 1984 passed the *New Zealand Nuclear Free Zone, Disarmament and Arms Control Act* in 1987, the world's first national nuclear-free legislation. Dr. Helen Caldicott's influence had culminated in the passage of the cornerstone of New Zealand's foreign policy.

MARILYN WARING is a New Zealand economist, feminist, author and activist. As a former politician, (she became a member of parliament at age 23), she played a key role in the passing of New Zealand's nuclear-free legislation, which is still a cornerstone of the country's foreign policy. Her hugely influential 1988 book, *If Women Counted,* was a revolutionary critique of the way the international standard of measuring economic growth discounts nature and women's unpaid labour.

GINN FOURIE

Ginn Fourie is a South African activist whose daughter was killed during apartheid. She works for reconciliation, peace and community building in South Africa and beyond, through various initiatives, including the Lyndi Fourie Foundation, which she co-founded with Letlapa Mphahlele, the man who masterminded the attack that killed her daughter.

FROM VICTIM TO WOUNDED HEALER

By Robi Damelin

In 1994, Ginn Fourie attended the trial of three men who had killed her 23-year-old daughter the previous year, and told them she forgave them. It was an early act of grace on Ginn's long, remarkable path to forgiveness and conciliation. Her journey would have far-reaching consequences not only for her but also for people throughout South Africa and beyond. Including me—a mother from Israel.

Ginn's daughter, Lyndi, was killed in the Heidelberg Tavern Massacre in the Cape Town suburb of Observatory, on New Year's Eve, 1993. A group of Freedom Fighters from the Azanian Peoples Liberation Army—the military wing of the Pan Africanist Congress—opened fire, shooting her at close range and killing three others. As Ginn later realized, Lyndi was not killed because she was Lyndi, but from anger over the injustices of apartheid and in revenge for the murder of five black schoolchildren by the South African Defense Forces just a month earlier. Lyndi, who had been studying civil engineering at the University of Cape Town, had always been sympathetic to the cause of black South Africans.

Forgiveness was not automatic for Ginn. When she first learned of Lyndi's death, the pain was acute: "It feels like your heart's being ripped right out of your chest," she once said of the days following her daughter's death. After the pain, she felt tremendous anger, some of which was directed at the perpetrators. But she saw soon enough that forgiveness was the only way to keep grief from overwhelming her. She turned to learning, studying the process of forgiveness and reconciliation in South Africa and working towards a doctorate in the subject. Eventually, Ginn came to a deep understanding of her own subtle prejudices and social role within the apartheid system.

Her journey of forgiveness included many stops along the way. On the day she sat in on the trial of her daughter's murderers— only a year after her death—Ginn was angry. But she did not feel hatred. She sent a message to them through an interpreter, saying that if they felt—or were—guilty, she forgave them. She relied on the judge to mete out justice, which he did, sentencing the men to 25 years in jail. In his sentence, the judge described them as "puppets" in a plot orchestrated by someone far more cunning and intelligent than they were.

After the trial, Ginn vowed to find the "intelligence" behind the attack on the Heidelberg Tavern, the people who she felt were really to blame for her loss. In 2002, she turned on her car radio to hear an interview with the man who admitted having organized the attack. His name was Letlapa Mphahlele. Ginn learned he was having a launch for a book he'd written, *Child of This Soil: My Life as a Freedom Fighter*. She decided to go to the event and confront him.

At the launch, Ginn put up her hand during the question-and-answer period, and explained who she was. She then accused Letlapa of trivializing South Africa's Truth and Reconciliation Commission—set up after the abolition of apartheid—by refusing to testify. Perpetrators of violence under the apartheid regime were allowed to testify to the commissioners and apply for amnesty from prosecution, but Letlapa had not done so. To Ginn's surprise, Letlapa responded openly to her accusation. He said he understood why it would appear he was trivializing the commission, then outlined his reasons for not participating. They included the fact that Azanian People's Liberation Army members were being held in prison at the time, while soldiers from the South African Defence Forces were not.

When the event finished, Letlapa came directly from the podium to ask Ginn if she would meet with him the following week. Seeing remorse in Letlapa's eyes, Ginn agreed. Slowly, the two began a dialogue. Over the following months, by working through skepticism on both sides, they formed an unlikely bond. Ginn gained a sense of respect for Letlapa's integrity and saw he truly wanted to build bridges between their communities. For his part, Letlapa was overwhelmed by Ginn's capacity for forgiveness. "By forgiving," he once told Ginn, "you have released me from the prison of my inhumanity."

Today, Letlapa and Ginn have progressed beyond their personal bond. They established the Lyndi Fourie Foundation to honour Ginn's daughter and provide a platform for bridge-building between communities. Their focus is on furthering conciliation in South Africa, bridging long-held differences and reducing local animosities. Their messages are being heard around the world, and they often travel to tell their story and share the lessons they've learned from one another.

Letlapa and Ginn's extraordinary story had a profound effect on me at a time when I needed it most. In 2002, my son David was killed as an act of revenge. A Palestinian sniper shot him. His death changed my life forever. Like Lyndi, David was a student when he was killed—studying for a master's in the philosophy of education. He was also one in a group of military officers who did not want to serve in the occupied territories. He had been in a quandary about serving in the military—Israel conscripts most young men and women—and discussed his dilemma with me. After much soul-searching, he decided to go into the military, saying that he would always treat people with dignity.

Life has taught me never to assume I'll know my enemy. Ginn's description of what it is to lose a child—like having your "heart ripped right out of your chest"—speaks to the dreadful physical and emotional pain I felt after David's death. I began to look for a way to prevent both Israeli and Palestinian families from experiencing that incredible pain. It was clear from the moment the soldiers came to tell me David had been killed—when I told them they could not kill anyone in the name of my child—that revenge would not be an option for me. But what was the right path? Like Ginn, I quickly understood the sniper had not killed David because he was David, but because he represented an occupying army. I learned later that when he was a small child, the sniper had seen his uncle violently killed by Israeli soldiers. He had also lost two other uncles in the second Intifada uprising. What a waste of life!

"Forgiveness," Ginn has said, "is part of moving from victim to survivor to wounded healer." Almost a year after David was killed, I met with bereaved Palestinian and Israeli families at a workshop organized by the Parents Circle-Families Forum. This grassroots organization is made up of more than 600 Israeli and Palestinian families, all of whom have lost an immediate family member to the conflict. We all work to humanize the "other side," to lay a foundation for reconciliation, which we feel is essential to long-term peace. When I participated in the Forum workshop that first time, I looked into the eyes of Palestinian mothers and realized that we shared the same pain. If we could harness that pain and speak with the same voice, then we could become a powerful force for change. "Vulnerable feelings, when expressed to other people," Ginn has said, "have the potential to establish lasting bonds." My new life started on that day, and I began the work I still do today: working toward reconciliation.

But even after I had started this work, I felt a void. I still did not know what forgiveness really meant for me. Had I truly succeeded in forgiving? Or indeed, *should* I forgive? The night Israeli soldiers told me they had caught the man who killed David, I felt even more lost. I did not want revenge, but I was even more confused about the role of forgiveness. Did it mean giving up my right to justice, or that the sniper could strike again? Was forgiving the same as forgetting my own child? I spoke to people from all religious backgrounds and found no satisfactory answers ...

Then I finally met Ginn. I spoke with her in her home when I went to South Africa to interview her for a documentary I was making. She was the first person I'd met who had lost a child but who could actually define what forgiveness meant for her. "I have come to understand," Ginn explained, "that forgiveness is a process which involves a principled decision to give up your justifiable right to revenge, for to accept it is a violation and a devaluation of self."

I had an emotional breakthrough. Ginn's definition of forgiveness is the only one that makes sense to me, and hearing it helped me understand the journey I was on. I may already have been on my way to forgiveness because I had never sought revenge. And I was working to help others heal. But now I understood that it was my love for David, as Ginn said, that had set me on this path. My forgiveness honours him—and gives me the courage to keep doing this work, one day at a time.

ROBI DAMELIN lost her son to a Palestinian sniper in 2002. Now, as the Director of the Women's Group for the Parents Circle-Families Forum in Israel, she promotes peace and reconciliation alongside other Israelis and Palestinians who have lost someone to the conflict.

RIGOBERTA MENCHÚ TUM

Rigoberta Menchú Tum is a life-long activist for Indigenous and women's rights who won the Nobel Peace Prize in 1992, and whose struggle to share with the world the history of oppression and violence against the Mayan people has made her an iconic global leader. In 2007 and 2011, she ran for president of Guatemala. She is a member of the board of Nobel Women's Initiative.

A DIGNIFIED JOURNEY FOR JUSTICE

By Pamela Yates

In 1983, I was a young woman travelling the world to screen my first feature-length documentary, *When the Mountains Tremble*, which told the story of the brutal violence then unfolding in Guatemala. I was not alone: Rigoberta Menchú Tum, the protagonist of the film, was travelling with me.

I remember Paris, in particular, where Rigoberta stood up after our screening and spoke to the packed theatre about the genocide being waged by the Guatemalan army against the Mayans— her people. It was a bloody campaign few in the audience had heard about. When Rigoberta spoke, her gentle voice engaged people by getting them to recognize their collective humanity, a philosophy that is key to Mayan culture and identity. By the end of the evening she had people committed to writing letters, speaking out, marching, donating funds and yearning for real change.

They'd never met anyone like her.

It is Rigoberta's ability to draw the full measure of potential from each and every person listening that is my enduring image of her. In her lifelong quest to first stop the violence in Guatemala, then to seek justice for the crimes that were committed during the decades-long civil war, Rigoberta became a formidable leader and one of the first Mayan women in history to be front and centre on a global stage.

Rigoberta's mother and father were local leaders, and taught her at a young age to respect and value her Mayan culture. Don Vicente Menchú was a Catholic catechist, or lay leader, who recognized his daughter's intelligence and innate ability to teach at an early age. He chose Rigoberta, the sixth of nine children, to walk with him from village to village in the Mayan highlands, so she could learn from him as he organized poor peasant farmers to recognize and fight for their rights. Doña Juana Tum, Rigoberta's mother, was a respected natural healer and midwife in their small highland village of Chimel. They were poor but lived richly, surrounded by the beauty of rivers and volcanic mountains, part of a vibrant, spiritual and ancient culture: the Maya-K'iche'.

The 1970s were a volatile time in Guatemala, when military dictators ruled and large landowners held total power. But farmers were defying authorities by organizing peasant cooperatives and creating a national peasant and Indigenous network: the Committee for Peasant Unity, or CUC, led by emerging leaders like Vicente Menchú. They learned to read and write and educated themselves about the factors that kept them poor. The Guatemalan government reacted with a ferociously repressive backlash. Peasants were killed or disappeared just for speaking out and practicing their rights.

In 1980, Vicente Menchú led a delegation of Mayan peasants and students in a nonviolent takeover of the Spanish Embassy in Guatemala City, in a bid to tell the world about the murders in the highlands. It was a hugely risky act of resistance, but the group felt they had no choice. They paid a high price for their defiance: the Guatemalan police attacked the embassy and set it on fire, killing 37 people, including Rigoberta's father. It was an attack that shocked the world.

Her father's murder devastated 21-year-old Rigoberta. A short time later, state security services kidnapped, raped and murdered her mother, Juana. Rather than withdraw into her grief, Rigoberta decided to act. She fled into hiding, first to a convent, then to Mexico, where liberation theologist Samuel Ruíz, the Bishop of Chiapas, took her in. Here, the gifts her father had nurtured in her—the abilities to teach, speak out and tell the world about the suffering of her people, inspiring them to act, would flourish.

For the next 10 years, Rigoberta criss-crossed the world, living out of a single suitcase—an exile driven by her intense desire to end the violence ravaging Guatemala. She says her mother Juana's spirit accompanied her. Rigoberta spoke out everywhere—in local churches, universities and community centres. She talked her way into government offices and even addressed the General Assembly at the United Nations. She became a selfless international spokesperson advocating peace and Indigenous rights, and heads of state began to take notice.

At the time Rigoberta was speaking at the U.N., I was in the midst of making my documentary, *When the Mountains Tremble*. A friend who knew about my film brought Rigoberta to my studio in New York City. I was struggling with how to tell the story of what was happening in Guatemala. I had filmed incredible, groundbreaking scenes there with army and guerrilla fighters, with civil society and the church, but had not yet found a way to hold them together. I conducted a filmed interview with Rigoberta and realized almost immediately that she had an extraordinary sense of vision. I brought her into the editing room and together we looked at all my filmed material. As the film rolled, she began telling the parallel story of her life, and I realized she had to be the storyteller for my film.

Rigoberta wrote her own story, weaving scenes together, then I filmed her speaking directly to the camera and—by extension—to the whole wide world. It was the first time the story of

Guatemala had ever been told from the unique perspective of a Mayan, let alone a Mayan woman.

When the Mountains Tremble premiered at the first Sundance Film Festival and was shown all over the world. It became part of the campaign to stop U.S. military intervention in Central America. The film helped put Rigoberta on the world stage and changed my life forever. Guatemala had wrapped its arms around my soul and would never let me go.

Ten years later, in 1992, Rigoberta was awarded the Nobel Peace Prize. This was the 500th anniversary of the arrival of Europeans in the Americas, a conquest that began in 1492 when their rapacious quest for land and gold unleashed a genocide against Indigenous peoples, from Canada to Tierra del Fuego, Chile's southern tip. The Nobel Peace Prize was awarded to Rigoberta "in recognition of her work for social justice and ethno-cultural reconciliation based on respect for the rights of indigenous peoples." She was the first Indigenous person and, at that time, the youngest person ever to receive the Nobel Peace Prize. As she rose to accept the award, she flashed the vibrant colors of her *güipil* and *corte*, the traditional Mayan dress, surrounded by a sea of Europeans dressed in neutral colors. Rigoberta told the gathering: "I consider this prize not as a reward to me personally, but rather as one of the greatest conquests in the struggle for peace, for human rights and for the rights of indigenous peoples, who, for 500 years, have been split, fragmented, as well as the victims of genocides, repression and discrimination."

But when you fight impunity, impunity fights back. In 1983, Rigoberta had published a book about her life. The book transformed the study and understanding of modern Guatemalan history. But after Rigoberta won the peace prize in 1992, her memoir also became a target for conservative historians and political figures in both Guatemala and the U.S. They sought to discredit Rigoberta's account and deny the genocidal campaign carried out by the Guatemalan military regime, with U.S. support. They tried to discredit her story by saying she lied about her own personal experiences, not understanding that she was writing the collective story of Indigenous peoples, which fits with the Mayan's ancestral, cosmovision philosophy. Some of her detractors even tried to get her Nobel Peace Prize rescinded but were rebuffed by the Nobel Committee. One internationally known academic described the Spanish Embassy attack that killed her father as an act of self-immolation by guerrilla subversives to gain attention for their cause. Rigoberta told me: "This charge made it feel like the victims, including my father, were being tortured and murdered over and over again."

She ignored these criticisms of her work, and continued on her path.

Using her international prestige as a Nobel laureate, Rigoberta launched a campaign to bring justice to the perpetrators of genocide in Guatemala. She was inspired by the Spanish National Court's issuing a warrant for the arrest of the Chilean General, Augusto Pinochet, on human rights charges, and went to the same court to build a case against those who had ordered the Spanish Embassy attack. The Spanish National Court claims universal jurisdiction, including the right to prosecute heinous crimes even if they take place in another country. As the Spanish Embassy case moved forward, emboldened judges and prosecutors in Guatemala obtained evidence from Spanish prosecutors and gathered the political will to bring the perpetrators to justice.

The Spanish Embassy trial began in Guatemala on October 1, 2014, and Rigoberta was the first person to testify. By January 2015, the chief of police, Pedro Arredondo, who had ordered the attack, was found guilty and sentenced to 40 years in prison. It was an emotional moment for Rigoberta and for all the surviving family members. People in the courtroom rose to their feet, crying out *"Justicia! Justicia! Justicia!"* Simply knowing that the historical record would now recount the true story of what had happened was empowering.

Rigoberta is helping to move justice forward in Guatemala

through other trials as well, including the case against a former president, General Efraín Ríos Montt. This historic trial ended in May 2013, after the Guatemalan court heard vivid testimony from survivors about the army's brutal scorched-earth policy in the Mayan highlands in 1982 and 1983. The court sentenced Ríos Montt, who came to power in a 1982 coup, to 80 years in prison for sanctioning the murders of 1,771 people, including children. Rigoberta's presence in the courtroom almost every day was a great support to the Maya-Ixil victims. Another case she supported was the Sepur Zarco sexual slavery trial. Fifteen Maya-Q'eqchi' women, who had been raped repeatedly, held against their will and forced to cook and clean for soldiers at the Sepur Zarco military base in the early 1980s, took two military officers to court. Again, Rigoberta lent her strong, dignified presence, listening to the women testify in 2016, during the first criminal trial for sexual slavery heard in a national court. And again, the accused were convicted successfully. The Mayan plaintiffs, now in their 50s and 60s, could finally celebrate some measure of justice.

Rigoberta isn't only about justice in the courtroom—she has dedicated her life to public service. In 2007, she founded the first political party led by Mayans, called WINAQ, which means "the whole person" in the K'iche' language. She has run for the presidency of Guatemala twice, the only Indigenous person to have done so. She ran to influence the national debate on the corruption of political parties as a corrosive force, weakening democracy. The WINAQ congressional representatives were among the first to investigate and denounce corruption at the highest government levels.

In 2012, Rigoberta was appointed to a specially endowed chair, named in her honour, at the Autonomous University of Mexico, one of the most prestigious universities in the Americas. Rigoberta now teaches human rights from an Indigenous perspective and researches structural discrimination. She helps shape public policy and the law so as to equalize the relationship of Indigenous people within a fully functioning democracy.

I have had the great pleasure of knowing Rigoberta Menchú for 34 years. We are now old friends and mature women or, as we like to joke, "*Somos viejas amigas y amigas viejas*" (we are old friends, and friends of old). And we continue to make films together. In 2011, we collaborated on *Granito: How to Nail a Dictator,* about building the Guatemalan genocide case against General Efraín Ríos Montt.

Rigoberta gave the film its title. When I asked her the meaning of the Mayan concept of *granito de arena*—a tiny grain of sand—she said: "It's a profoundly humble phrase. It means to say: I alone can't change things, but I can help to change things. It's a collective concept of change. It's revolutionary because it signifies a process, that the struggle can take many forms. Change comes through struggle. And a grain of sand is a strong philosophy that unites collective rights and individual rights. Because what I give is only a contribution—a grain of sand—but the sands are vast. For me there are no heroes; no one is more heroic than another. And when destiny calls, you have to act."

Rigoberta's life-long commitment to act has changed Guatemala. It has changed the world.

PAMELA YATES is an award-winning documentary filmmaker and human rights activist from the U.S. Her highly acclaimed 1983 film, *When the Mountains Tremble,* tells the story of Guatemala's internal armed conflict through the personal life and struggles of Rigoberta Menchú Tum. Yates' 2011 film, *Granito: How to Nail a Dictator,* is the sequel to *When the Mountains Tremble* and tells the story of the building a genocide case against General Efraín Ríos Montt.

DING ZILIN

A professor of philosophy and aesthetics, Ding Zilin founded the organization Tiananmen Mothers after her 17-year-old son was shot by government troops—alongside an unknown number of others—during peaceful democracy protests in Tiananmen Square in 1989. Tiananmen Mothers is comprised of relations of those killed on the night of June 3 and in the early morning of June 4, 1989, and seeks truth and accountability from the Chinese government for the massacre.

THE RIGHT TO GRIEVE

By Madeleine Thien

It is dusk. Birds in flight returning,
travellers setting out — it never ends.

Wang Wei

In 1989, Ding Zilin lived a relatively ordinary life, even a fortunate one. Alongside her husband, Jiang Peikun, she taught at People's University in Beijing, where both were highly regarded professors of philosophy and aesthetics. They had come of age in, and survived, the catastrophic political campaigns of Mao Zedong's China, which, in just over 25 years, had taken the lives of 60 million people.[1] They had a son, Jiang Jielian.

That year, the Tiananmen demonstrations began. The catalyzing

---

[1] "All the estimates of the innocent dead are mind boggling," Edward Friedman and Roderick Mac-Farquhar, Introduction to *Tombstone: The Great Chinese Famine*, 1958-1962 (New York: Farrar, Straus and Giroux, 2012) by Yang Jisheng, who puts the dead in these four years alone at 36 million. In *Mao's Great Famine: The Story of China's Most Devastating Catastrophe* (London: Bloomsbury, 2010), historian Frank Dikötter puts the death toll for 1958-1962 at 45 million. For the entirety of Mao Zedong's 27 years in power (1949-1976), "How Many Died: New Evidence Suggests Far Higher Numbers for Victims of Mao Zedong's Era", Valerie Strauss and Daniel Southerland, *The Washington Post*, July 17, 1994, estimates are between 40 and 120 million.

event was as simple as it was unexpected: the sudden death of Hu Yaobang, a Communist Party leader widely admired for his economic reforms. Two years earlier, Hu had been accused of soft-pedalling the government's response to the pro-democracy movement; disgraced, he had been removed from power. In April 1989, in the lead up to Hu's funeral, Tiananmen Square suddenly became a garden of flowers, poems and songs. The night before the funeral, over 100,000 students slept on the ground in order to preempt the government's decision to close the Square to the public during the ceremony.

One week later, the government declared the actions of the students—their public display of grief over the passing of Hu Yaobang—a threat to national security.

The government's hard line brought a massive, unprecedented response on behalf of the students. For the next six weeks, continuous protests would draw up to a million people—students, journalists, factory workers, police officers, waitresses, bankers, scientists and more—into Tiananmen Square every day, filling the space so tightly that, in Ding Zilin's words, "not even a drop of water could get through." Her son, Jielian, still in high school, was among them, carrying a banner of support: "Even if you fall, we will still be here." Around him, his fellow citizens were voicing desires that had been suppressed for decades: "Is it not time to live like human beings?"; "Why is it that we can't choose our own jobs?"; "What right does the government have to keep a private file on me?"; "A sincere and honest man has died, but the hypocritical live on." On May 13th, thousands of Beijing university students began a hunger strike, asking, "If not us, then who?"

Jielian had been born in 1972, the same year as my older sister. He was, his mother says, an idealist and a voracious reader who wanted to read "ten lines at a glance." When a book came into the house that all three family members wanted to read, they would take it apart in three sections, one for each. After everyone had finished, they would stitch the book back together again. During the Tiananmen demonstrations, Jielian's father, concerned for his son's safety, followed him to the Square and, from a nearby street, watched over him all night.

On the evening of June 3rd, 1989, Jielian went out to join the protests. Three hours later, as he tried to hide behind a raised flowerbed, he was shot in the chest by soldiers from the People's Liberation Army. His mother writes, "He was dead in an instant." Two days passed before his parents, reeling between hope and despair, recovered the body of their 17-year-old son. On June 5, with his body still bleeding from the gunshot wound, Ding Zilin kissed her son goodbye.

"Since arriving in this world," Ding Zilin wrote years later, "I had only wanted to live an ordinary life."[2] She was born, grew up, and married in a time when Mao and the Communist Party had plunged China into years of violent revolution. Under Mao, 60 million deaths pulled apart families, security, faith, dreams and selfhood; they comprise a vast, troubled sea lying in wait beneath all acts of public remembrance in China.

After a period of unbearable grief and guilt at the loss of her child, in which she tried several times to take her own life, Ding Zilin decided, in 1991, to ask for something very simple: the right to mourn peacefully and in public.

Together, she and another bereaved mother, Zhang Xianling, gave an interview to ABC News. Zhang Xianling's son, Wang Nan, had also been a high school student. He was shot at close range and subsequently denied medical treatment and comfort from volunteer medics as, for three hours, he lay on the ground,

---

[2] Ding Ziling, "Born Into Challenges, Dead in an Instant," translated by Human Rights in China and published online July 25, 2014. http://hrichina.org/en/china-rights-forum/born-challenges-dead-instant-part-1

dying. When she finally found her son's body, Zhang Xianling was issued a stamped receipt with her son's name and cause of death, "Shot outside and died."

Then and now, the Chinese government maintains that the dead were merely hooligans and counter-revolutionaries. Indeed, according to them, most of the deaths—estimated to be in the hundreds, and perhaps thousands—did not occur at all. In the aftermath of the ABC interview, they began a campaign of harassment and intimidation against Ding Zilin and Zhang Xianling. In response, the two women founded the Tiananmen Mothers; searching for others who shared the same fate, they looked for friendship and comfort. Their demand was simple and heart-wrenching—the right to grieve.

For these families, history will never be a closed book. Today, thirteen people arrested during the 1989 demonstrations are in prison. Just before the 23rd anniversary, a man named Ya Weilin committed suicide. His son, Ai Guo (whose name means "to love one's country"), had been 22 years old when he was killed on June 3rd. In his suicide note, Ya Weilin wrote, "There is still no justice." On the 25th anniversary, for the first time, Beijing residents holding a private Tiananmen memorial in their apartment were arrested and charged. The very spot where Zhang Xianling's son was killed has been equipped with a government surveillance camera: a camera meant for her alone. Through these devices, the police, too, remember and attempt to revise the book of history.

Twenty-seven years later, the Tiananmen Mothers, "this group of old people,"[3] pose the greatest threat to what journalist Louisa Lim has called *The People's Republic of Amnesia*. For nearly three decades, the founders of the Tiananmen Mothers have been subjected to 24-hour surveillance. Ding Zilin and

---

[3] Zhang Xianling, interviewed by Louisa Lim in *The People's Republic of Amnesia*, 2014.

Zhang Xianling are routinely arrested without charge, trailed by as many as 40 police officers as they buy their groceries, and denounced to friends and colleagues. Their computers, phones and belongings are seized. In the months around the June 4th anniversary, they are placed under arrest, held captive, and prohibited outside contact. They are either escorted by police each time they wish to visit the cemetery—or prevented from doing so altogether. Ding Zilin's name is blocked on the Chinese Internet, as are the words *jì niàn* 纪念 (to remember).

And yet, the Tiananmen Mothers have collected the names of 202 people killed that night—an extraordinary achievement in the face of the most politically sensitive and censored event in Chinese history. Their members continue to care for one another as family, to provide material and financial assistance, to record testimonies and to support one another publicly. They steadfastly ask for something so heartbreakingly simple: to weep, to speak.

Political acts undertaken in memory of love have an immeasurable resonance. They survive.

***

In 2002, my mother died suddenly after being discharged from a Canadian hospital. That week, I saw a woman standing on a subway platform. Her daughter, around five or six years old, was leaning against her, and the woman rested her palms on her child's shoulders. The woman was weeping openly. In my own distress, I too began to sob. The circumstances of my mother's death would never be resolved; indeed, the hospital, fearing a lawsuit, would not speak to us and, for over a year, refused to release any documents relating to her treatment. The devastation I felt was inexpressible. I watched the mother and child and, in public, poured out my sorrow. I was 28 years old. I was free to cry, shout and demand answers: the freedom to grieve is one I will never take for granted.

This year, Ding Zilin is 81 years old. The persistence of her love for her son, as well as her love for the families of the dead and missing of Tiananmen, inspires me year after year, as a writer and as a daughter. In my life, I have chosen literature as the means to pull open the book of history—to divide it, distribute it and sew it back together again—so that I might learn how to live truthfully in the brevity we are granted. "I know I am not a very bold mother," Ding Zilin says. "I do not have endurance. I do not speak beautiful, inspiring words. But on the path to fight for human rights, to demand justice, I have kept my endurance and keep on my way. This might be another way of living."

MADELEINE THIEN is the author of three novels and one short-story collection. Her most recent novel, *Do Not Say We Have Nothing*, examines the legacy of the decade-long Cultural Revolution and the 1989 Tiananmen demonstrations through the multi-generational story of a family of classically-trained musicians.

JODY WILLIAMS

Jody Williams won the Nobel Peace Prize in 1997 for her work on the International Campaign to Ban Landmines. The Chair of Nobel Women's Initiative, Williams travels the world advocating for human rights—particularly self-determination and women's rights. She is globally recognized for her contributions to peace and security, including through a current campaign to ban killer robots. In 2013 she published *My Name is Jody Williams: A Vermont Girl's Winding Path to the Nobel Peace Prize.*

SHE FIGHTS FROM THE HEART

By Audrey Wells

When Jody Williams was seven years old, she declared to her parents that when she grew up, she was going to be Pope. It was a rather shocking thing to announce to her devout Catholic parents, and contained not a small amount of hubris. Furthermore, it was, of course, an unattainable dream. Laughable. In fact, she might as well have said, "Mom and Dad, when I grow up, I'm going to win the Nobel Peace Prize."

Which she did. Forty years later.

From a very tender age, Jody Williams had no qualms about trying to accomplish the impossible. One might say that she was born with more than her share of vision. But knowing Jody as I do—meaning both as a friend, and as a filmmaker—I would say that it's not vision that fuels Jody but something else, something that lives in the belly. Something closer to fire, to grit. Rage over injustice roils inside Jody like stomach acid. Jody acts from her gut, punches from the shoulder, fights from the heart and leads with her intellect. She's an unstoppable force who travels the world waging peace, until she collapses, exhausted, and returns to her beloved husband, her loyal dog and cats, and her cheese fondue pot. That's home.

Jody was the leader of the International Campaign to Ban Landmines from 1992 to 1997, the year that 122 countries signed the Mine Ban Treaty in an unprecedented act of cooperation between nations, citizens and non-governmental organizations from around the world. Because of the movement that Jody led, these many nations agreed to cease manufacturing, stock piling, trading and using landmines. They also agreed to cooperate on a massive initiative to dig up and disarm the millions of land mines left in the ground that continue to kill and maim innocent people around the world, dozens of years after their war is over. The Mine Ban Treaty has saved millions of lives and countless limbs, and will continue to do so, far into the future.

For coordinating this global act of peace, Jody Williams won the Nobel Peace Prize in 1997. She was 47 years old. You would think that this achievement and honour would have made Jody a national treasure and an American hero, whose name was familiar to schoolchildren across the land. Not the case. This can be explained in part by the fact that the United States has refused to sign the treaty. Jody had a protracted battle with the Clinton Administration over the issue. Indeed, on the day that Jody was award the Peace Prize, Jody called President Bill Clinton "a weenie" for not signing the ban. Her remark appeared on the front page of the *New York Times*.

Cut to black.

Jody doesn't care that she's not a household name in the United States. She comes from a working class background where people value you for what you do, not for how you appear, or how much fame or glory you have. She was born to a loving, working class family in Vermont, with two sisters and two brothers. Her mother, Ruth, worked at home raising the children and caring for her oldest son, who was born deaf.

Jody's father, John, drove a coal-delivery truck, until later he started his own vending machine business. Jody worked for her father for a spell, making the ham sandwiches that went into those vending machines.

After getting a degree at the University of Vermont and divorcing her high school sweetheart, the sandwich-maker wasn't sure what she wanted to do with her life. Jody decided to pursue another degree to enable her to teach both English as a second language, and Spanish.

One morning, in 1981, Jody found a way to put her Spanish to work. Riding the Metro to work—she'd taken a job teaching remedial English to new immigrants in Washington, D.C.—a man handed her a pamphlet that changed everything. It said: "El Salvador: Another Vietnam?" The flyer talked about ending the war in El Salvador, and invited anyone and everyone to attend an informational meeting in a church basement. Jody walked down those basement stairs, sat in the meeting, and got that burning feeling in her gut that's guided so many of her life-altering decisions, before and since.

Signing up with Medical Aid for El Salvador, an American non-governmental organization, Jody took delegations of Americans carrying medical supplies to El Salvador so they could see firsthand the impact of the U.S.-sponsored war in that country. Her job also entailed travelling into bombed-out villages, earning the trust of countless war-affected El Salvadoran families, and arranging airlifts to transport the wounded children to the United States, where they could receive the medical attention they needed. It was dangerous work in a war zone, and eventually Jody became a victim herself. A death squad operative paid her hotel room a visit, and asked her to leave the country—by raping her.

Jody refused to leave El Salvador and carried on with her

work until burnout eventually forced her to retreat back to D.C. What followed for Jody was a period of self-doubt. But soon Medico International—a group that had helped support some of her work in El Salvador—and the Vietnam Veterans of America Foundation, came to her with a proposal. Would Jody consider working as their organizer, to coordinate an international ban on land mines? It would involve thousands of hours of international travel, endless meetings, relentless work, exhaustive negotiations, no family holidays, pathetic pay and zero guarantees. Of course, Jody said "yes."

Seven years later, the sandwich-maker from Vermont was holding a Nobel Peace Prize. Jody Williams is living proof that indeed, one person with a passion can make a difference.

Today, Jody and her husband, Steve Goose, are working to ban another class of weapons: "killer robots," fully autonomous weapons. As a longtime head of the arms division of Human Rights Watch, Goose (as Jody calls him) helped to co-found the International Campaign to Ban Landmines—which is where he and Jody met. Together, they give new meaning to the term "power couple." Nothing slows them down.

The last time I saw Jody, she had come to Los Angeles to speak at Peace Jam—an international education program built around Nobel Peace Prize Laureates, who work personally with youth to pass on the spirit, skills, and wisdom they embody. I claimed Jody's few free hours for myself, and picked her up at her hotel to take her out to dinner. Before we walked into the restaurant, Jody stopped under a streetlight, saying she wanted to introduce me to the latest addition to her family. I raised my eyebrows, wondering who that might be, and how I could possibly meet this new person, right then, on a street corner in Beverly Hills. That's when Jody unbuttoned the top button on her pants, and pulled down the waistband to show me a brilliantly colored, brand new tattoo across her lower abdomen. The tattoo was of a dragon; beautifully executed, it snaked gracefully over her belly, covering a new hysterectomy scar. "Her name is Raven," she said, smiling like a farm girl from Vermont. "Don't you think she's cute?"

To me, this story epitomizes Jody. It exemplifies the way she's lived her life. If you fall down, if you lose, if you get hurt—don't whine about it. Tattoo it. Slap a big, bad-ass, dragon over the whole damn thing. Proclaim your intentions to the world. Stay. Fight. Breathe fire.

And carry on.

AUDREY WELLS is an award-winning American screenwriter and filmmaker. Her films, such as *Guinevere* and *Under the Tuscan Sun*, often explore complex heroines.

MARCELA LAGARDE Y DE LOS RIOS

Marcela Lagarde y de los Ríos is one of Mexico's most influential feminists. An anthropologist, academic and former politician, Lagarde is credited with introducing the concept of *femicide*—the systematic disappearance and killing of women, in which the state is complicit either directly or by perpetrating impunity for such crimes—to Latin America. Her research on femicides contributed to the Inter-American Court of Human Rights verdict in 2009 against Mexico for its failure to protect hundreds of women in Ciudad Juarez.

SISTERHOOD AND PEACE

By Lydia Cacho

The year was 1993, and women of all ages packed a room. I had just turned 30, and I felt a great sense of anticipation. The round tables, placed in a circle, seemed to form a perfect mandala. Before us stood a woman with long black hair, dressed in purple traditional Mexican clothing, smiling with her mouth and face at the same time. There was something inscrutable about this renowned Mexican feminist anthropologist, and we all wanted to learn her secret. How did she manage to see the world with such empathy, yet maintain her unique scientific perspective: one rooted in feminist philosophy? Marcela Lagarde y de los Ríos had asked us to bring photographs from our childhood, of our mothers, grandmothers and aunts. Some of us brought boxes of pictures, others only one or two.

During this workshop, which lasted two full days, Marcela led our diverse group of a hundred women (activists, academics, students, journalists, lawyers, housewives, Indigenous women and city-dwellers) step-by-step on a voyage into our ancestral pasts. She guided us as—together—we reconstructed the history of women in our country. Above all, Marcela took each of us by the hand and explained the keys to understanding feminine ideology. How, when, where and who had taught us to be the women we were in our own eyes, in the eyes of others, in men's eyes—and behind their backs? From whom did we learn (perhaps in childhood) to use violence or, in contrast, to negotiate conflict without violence or to use (that more subtle form of aggression) manipulation?

Our encounter became a trip down the intricate pathways of the psyche. How can I know who I am? Or, what is the point of being an activist if I don't understand how I am violent myself, or how I deal with acts of violence by others? Marcela asked that question again and again over the two days. Cultivating leadership consists, above all, in daring to navigate the entrails of our own ideologies, personae—our essences as women. Those innards determine how we function in society and why we give ourselves over to certain causes, powers, people—and to love or to war.

How do women view leadership? According to Marcela Lagarde y de los Ríos, we women who get into politics lack our own names for the things that we really want. Instead, we adopt the patriarchal language of war and imposition. Unless we invent our own ways of naming desirable goals or things, we cannot reinvent the world.

To understand the current state of Latin American women's movements, we need both to grasp their diversity and decide whether we truly want to build a peaceful world based on justice and equality for all. Forms of leadership created by women, Marcela insists, are engaging because they come from inside, emanating from the heart, from what we are physically and what we desire. The vast majority of activist women work against violence (to people, animals and nature) because they understand the damage violence does to living things. But they also aspire to a more peaceful world, where egalitarian societies make sure every person has access to food, water, health and happiness. Even if happiness is intermittent, everyone has a right to experience prosperity and joy. Marcela says that where violence prevails, some people might enjoy power, but real happiness in such places does not exist.

Marcela Lagarde y de los Ríos has written some 20 texts on anthropology and feminism—an essential canon in the Spanish-speaking world—and is a principal proponent of feminist pacifism in Latin America. She has trained thousands of women and men in her lifetime. Her teaching techniques combine solid science with accessible, effective practice, and active listening with learning from collective experience.

Her workshop taught us the key characteristics of feminist leadership, two in particular. The first is that our leaders work through persuasion. Women the world over, despite being marginalized and suffering inequality, nevertheless seek not to impose their views but to convince, and they usually achieve lasting results that benefit broad sectors within their communities and wider societies. The history of feminist leadership is marked by milestone attempts to change a mistrustful world, one that discredits women's words, above all when we propose radical changes in gender relations. Despite such mistrust, women are firm, consistent and persistent advocates. According to Marcela, women today carry on the traditions of the Enlightenment. Women leaders try to bring knowledge to light through argument, using reason, which we must assume is universal.

The second most crucial aspect of feminist leadership is that we win ideological debates by supplementing discussion with precise, concerted and collective actions. Intellectual and community leadership by women tends to be active and leads by example. There are millions of extraordinary women leaders working around the world in communities large and small. Women activists, Marcela says, are attempting something amazing and new: to take an idea of the world we want to live in and turn it into life itself. We seek to transform utopian ideals into cornerstones of personal and collective practice. Every woman leader, using the ideas she has internalized, translates into lived experience the alternatives she desires for the world. This nexus of thinking, being, existing and feeling is crucial to our leadership.

Historically, the leadership of men has typically depended on charismatic individuals—and gains coherence not by combining thinking and living but by imposing rules and obeying them, by accumulating wealth and being respected for having it. Today's women pose an epistemological paradigm shift by seeking to apply utopian propositions to the ways we live every day.

Marcela Lagarde y de los Ríos is a feminist who incorporates a unique perspective of peace into every aspect of her teaching. She travels with and encourages feminist women and men as they deepen their relationship with each other, as they unravel the flaws they inherited when their gender identity was constructed, as they assess how and when they formulated (perhaps in their youth) their ideas about power, leadership and equality.

This Mexican doctor of anthropology, ethnologist, feminist, mother of three sons and a daughter, activist and professor, who turned 68 in 2016, has strengthened the linkage between idealism and activism. Twenty-two years ago I learned from her own lips that one of feminism's greatest contributions to humanity is to put ethics before politics, because ethics both prefigures and configures politics. From Marcela I learned that gender inequities in Latin America are part of our national political culture. Simply proclaiming gender equality or even enacting legislation to ensure it does not necessarily transform the lives of women, educational norms or cultural stereotypes. I also discovered that, in practice, big "D" Democracy and Development were not formulated or planned to include women as protagonists in history. Democracy was conceived by men—even though women marched alongside them to achieve it.

Now we face an even more arduous challenge: to build peace on a new foundation, through the critical revision of the modern concept of democracy. We must be capable of questioning long-held assumptions such as *adultocracy* that mistreats girls and boys and conceives of them as objects rather than as living beings with natural rights. Peace, Marcela tells us, must be built on a foundation of critical and congruent leadership. Never before have the women of the world been so interconnected: Africans, Latin Americans, Europeans, Asians, Australians and Nordics are, for the first time in human history, working together across gender identities in all kinds of human endeavours. Today, more than ever before, women enjoy a paradigmatic connection, involving feelings, philosophies, life practices and concrete actions, each echoing and supporting others.

That is how women—young mavericks and elder sages, adult women and girls—are building peace as we reinvent the world. Thanks to teachers like Marcela Lagarde y de los Ríos, many of us have decided to take to the loudspeaker and enter the spotlight, becoming role models and lighting the way, offering home and safe harbours for those women and men who also dream of a world where equality and justice are the twin pillars of peace, and where peace delivers well-being, diversity and happiness.

LYDIA CACHO is one of Mexico's most prominent investigative journalists. Cacho's writing is primarily focused on violence against and sexual abuse of women and children. She has won a number of international awards for her work, including Amnesty International's Ginetta Sagan Award for Women and Children's Rights and the Oxfam/Novib Pen Award.

NATALYA ESTEMIROVA

Natalya Estemirova was an internationally renowned Russian journalist who reported regularly on human rights abuses in Chechnya. She was also a board member of the human rights organization Memorial, and was a regular consultant for Human Rights Watch. In 2009, Estemirova was abducted and murdered.

ARMED ONLY WITH A DICTAPHONE

By Anna Nemtsova

On a sunny Tuesday in July 2009, I received a phone call from a friend in Grozny, Chechnya. My friend sounded frightened. The news was not only bad but it touched me personally, and was sadly predictable. "They abducted Natasha right from the courtyard of her house!"

Natalya Estemirova, the great-hearted 51-year-old Russian human rights defender, known to her many friends and colleagues as "Natasha," had been grabbed violently by four gunmen as she left her house that morning. With terrified neighbours looking on, the men bundled Natasha into an unmarked white car and sped away.

Later that day, another call brought me the tragic outcome: "They killed her."

I learned that her abductors had driven Natasha from Chechnya to the neighboring republic of Ingushetia. Her body was found there the same afternoon. She lay at the side of a road, her face beaten and her hands tied, with bullet wounds to her head and chest.

As a Russian journalist covering violence, corruption and oppression in the region, I had come to know Natasha personally as a tireless advocate for justice. She had been an invaluable guide who quickly became a friend. When I travelled to Grozny to report on the troubled situation there, Natasha would invite me and my fellow journalists to stay in her home.

Natasha lived with her teenaged daughter, Lana, in a tiny two-bedroom apartment on the top floor of a nine-storey building. There was no running water and the elevator didn't work. I remember the first time she showed us around, she pointed to a huge shrapnel hole in the wall separating her daughter's bedroom from the hallway. "Check out the new ventilation," she said, her dry sense of humour lifting the mood. "I never have time to fix it, so now it's part of our interior design." A human rights activist in a place that desperately needs them, Natasha had bigger issues to deal with than her own creature comforts.

As a young woman, Natasha had earned a university degree in history and became a history teacher. She had a husband who died during the first Chechen war against the Russian federation, which started in 1994. The war, which was wildly unpopular with the Russian public, eventually ended in 1996. After her husband's death, Natasha began to work as a correspondent for local newspapers and for television, reporting on or filming documentaries about the victims of Russian government abuses. Although she continued teaching for several years, Natasha had now started down a different path. "That was when I became a human rights activist at heart. When my husband died in the war, my heart hardened." That was all she ever told me about that part of her personal life. She didn't like to talk about what happened to her husband, but I understood that losing him was part of what drove her to expose the oppression, abductions and torture condoned by Russian leaders.

In the days following her abduction, I asked myself and other journalists and activists: *who ordered Natasha's murder?*

Natasha's colleagues at Memorial, the Russian historical and civil rights society where she worked, believed and publicly declared that the head of the Chechen Republic, Ramzan Kadyrov, was behind the crime. Kadyrov is a very controversial figure in the region, and has been regularly linked in media reports to numerous vicious human rights violations, theft of public funds and protecting criminals.

Two years before her murder, Natasha had accepted a position as head of a civil society advisory commission for the Chechen capital, Grozny, presided over by President Kadyrov. While fulfilling her role as advisor to local government, however, she continued filing reports for Memorial, many of which exposed Kadyrov's oppressive policies and the violent methods used to enforce them. One report she wrote, which was about Kadyrov's decision to forbid girls to attend university without wearing headscarves, made him particularly angry. He summoned Natasha to a city office, screamed at her for questioning policy, then fired her from the advisory committee. Kadyrov threatened her several times, she later told me.

But Natasha never stopped writing about Kadyrov and his government. Rushing around with her laptop and a dictaphone, she worked with dogged determination. She and her colleagues at Memorial documented and publicized 76 cases of abduction in 2009 alone, a jump from the 35 cases they had uncovered the previous year. Overall, Memorial monitors have documented some 5,000 cases of people who have disappeared since the start of the first Chechen war in 1994. Natasha called it an "abduction epidemic," a scourge personally endorsed by Kadyrov.

I once called Natasha from Moscow to learn more. "Come and see for yourself," she told me. "The bandits are shooting us

Chechens like rabbits." She was not afraid to express such views publicly, and her defiance infuriated the thuggish Chechen leader.

On the day I learned of Natasha's murder, I flew to Chechnya to attend her funeral. I could not stop thinking of the horror and pain she must have suffered in her last few hours of life. She had used previously her historian's training to graphically describe the Chechen abduction cases to me, so I could hear Natasha's own voice describing her final hours. Many of the cases she wrote about directly paralleled her own: an abductee pushed into a car by men in civilian clothes or by militants, in full view of witnesses.

Many people feel hopeless about the search for justice in today's Russia, where the government's critics lose jobs, go to jail or are abducted and killed. But Natasha never lost hope in the face of these dangers. Rather, it was her chosen mission to expose such threats and try to influence positive change.

Natasha also knew the kind of powers she was up against. Kadyrov was president Vladimir Putin's favourite governor, a loyalist who was afforded endless authority and forgiven all violations.

Natasha once told me in an interview I conducted with her for *Newsweek*, that "[t]he Kremlin gave a green light to the special service and local militia to do as they please here, on the condition that they provide Chechnya's absolute loyalty to Russia."

Another time, Natasha and I stayed up all night in her kitchen, talking about how the Kremlin ignored the violence perpetrated in Chechnya by Kadyrov's men. The men were terrifying people to the point where most had become afraid even to speak to human rights activists like Natasha. That night in particular, I was struck by the contrasts reflecting the broader situation in Chechnya. There were Natasha and her daughter living in a time-worn building with no running water, working to improve people's lives, while Kadyrov the oppressor resided in a luxurious residence with his own private zoo.

Today, Kadyrov also has a palace, with a marble and faux-gold interior, palm trees and enormous portraits of President Putin hanging on the walls.

"Who killed Natasha?" I asked Kadyrov myself in 2014, on the eve of the Sochi Olympics, when I interviewed him at the palace. "My haters, those who want to undermine my reputation, all the great work I have done for Chechnya," he answered. Yet I was told he prevented any real investigation into Natasha's murder from taking place.

Since Natasha was murdered, the flood of victims applying for Memorial's help to find missing loved ones has slowed to a trickle. Only families who have lost almost all hope of ever seeing a loved one again are desperate enough to ask human rights defenders for help. It is a last resort. Memorial's office sits empty most of the time, though Natasha's colleagues refuse to stop working. By doing so, they are taking serious risks: their profession is a lethally dangerous one in Natasha's home republic. In the last two years, Russian authorities have been condemning civic groups like Memorial as "foreign agents," for accepting Western grants to continue their work.

The few remaining non-governmental organizations in Chechnya experience constant attacks from Kadyrov and his henchmen. In 2014, lawyers from the Joint Mobile Group with the Committee for the Prevention of Torture, which investigates allegations of state-sanctioned torture and abuses, halted activities after their office was set on fire and employees were threatened.

If Natasha were still with us, I can imagine her sitting up straight, shaking that thick, shiny mane and pronouncing in her determined way: "Something needs to be done about this urgently." And then she would get straight to work, motivating others to join her. People said that Natasha could get the dead to rise and walk for a good cause.

I heard recently from Mobile Group lawyers that they had moved into Natasha's former home, where the shrapnel hole still yawns. It seems fitting that the apartment now hosts young people from different regions of Russia who devote themselves to helping victims of torture, even as frightened, oppressed Chechens eschew help from the few remaining human rights groups.

In the current climate, not many Russian women would understand Natasha. Why would a single mother pass up political asylum in Western Europe to live on the top floor of a building with a permanently broken elevator and a water bottle apparatus for a shower?

Those of us close to her knew that Natasha had been conflicted for weeks before her abduction about what to do with her life: whether to stay in Chechnya and continue helping those who suffered injustices, or leave and start a new life with Lana, in a safer place. In today's Russia, most people choose to escape the country after a first warning, not wait for threats to take definite shape.

Natasha had tried to take breaks from Chechnya—twice she attempted to establish a different life for her daughter and herself in Europe. But each time, she could not stop herself from returning to her troubled homeland to report on torture, abductions and killings. She had pursued many of her investigations for years and was committed to seeing them through. Natasha followed one simple rule: she never gave up an investigation until she knew for certain that nothing else could be done.

Natasha was so much more than a driven activist. She was a compassionate human being. At Natasha's funeral in the

Chechen village of Koshkeldy, I met with a heartbroken woman named Deshi Inderbiyeva. Inderbiyeva wept like a child on the veranda of the house where we said goodbye to Natasha. She told me a story about a Russian military force burning her sister alive in 2000. Inderbiyeva was pregnant when this horror took place and so traumatized, she gave birth prematurely to a disabled boy. Inderbiyeva shared with me a detail that says much about Natasha. "Just a few days before she was murdered, Natasha came to visit us," she said. "Knowing how poor we are, she bought a school bag and books for my son. We lost a merciful angel!"

As we said goodbye to Natasha that day, Lana told us: "I do not want to see my mother's dead body. In my memory she will always be the strongest and most alive person in the world. My mother was killed for confronting the war against peaceful people."

In 2015, I was honoured to receive the Courage in Journalism Award from the International Women's Media Foundation. I wish that I could share the award with Natasha. When I reread her unfiltered documentation of torture, abductions and extrajudicial killings in Russia, I know that she was the most courageous woman I will ever meet.

ANNA NEMTSOVA is a reporter based in Moscow. She has been published in *Foreign Policy, The Washington Post, The Guardian,* and *Al Jazeera,* among others. She is also a correspondent for *Newsweek* and *The Daily Beast.* In 2015, Anna won the International Women's Media Foundation's Courage in Journalism Award.

LEYMAH GBOWEE

Leymah Gbowee won the Nobel Peace Prize in 2011 for her work leading a women's peace movement that brought the Second Liberian Civil War to an end. She travels the world speaking to audiences about gender-based violence and women-led peacebuilding in conflict countries. She is the founder and president of the Gbowee Peace Foundation Africa, a co-founder of the Women's Peace and Security Network Africa, and is on the board of directors of Nobel Women's Initiative.

LESSONS FROM A PEACEMAKING (S)HERO

By Danai Gurira

Ilearned my first lesson from Nobel Peace Prize winner, Leymah Gbowee, long before I ever met her.

Be bold

There is a naked boldness to Leymah. Anyone who has spent a minute in her presence knows this. But boldness is hard-won, earned through expressing a fierce heart in dire circumstances, through daring to be unpopular, through standing in defiance. Leymah's boldness consists of sheer grit, determination and, at its very core, a lot of hope and love.

Leymah's story is one most would find hard to believe. She tells it beautifully and viscerally in her autobiography, *Mighty Be our Powers: How Sisterhood, Prayer, and Sex Changed a Nation at War*. Leymah was born and brought up in a middle-class home in Monrovia, Liberia, before her world was torn apart by a vicious civil war. She was separated from family, witnessed unspeakable brutality, and lived in squalid conditions and constant, dire danger. While she mothered five children, she became the victim of domestic violence. Her return to her parents' home, once she managed to leave her abuser, was not joyous. She battled depression and poverty and saw no future for herself. Then her true calling came knocking at the door.

To tell one's story publicly, to let the world know what you have endured, along with all your imperfections, takes real courage. And courage, as we all know, is not always easily found.

As a playwright, I often encounter young women writers afraid to release the burden on their hearts and tell their stories for fear of the world's unfavourable response. A woman must be bold to manifest her vision of the world. This is our mission—response be damned. Or we conspire in silencing ourselves.

I came to Leymah's story through the documentary *Pray the Devil Back to Hell*, which recounts how five women in Liberia—including Leymah—brought an end to civil war in their country. They reached across religious and ethnic divides to work for peace with women traditionally on the "other side." I know the film back to front because it is the basis for my play, *Eclipsed*. I have watched it countless times with artists whom I wish to transform through the heart and soul of Liberia before we attempt to portray Liberia and its women in my play. Some people gravitate toward a superhero like Batman or Spiderman; those dudes have nothing on Leymah. To watch how she fights for peace is to know what true courage is: what *superSheroism* is.

Leymah led thousands of Christian and Muslim women of Liberia in almost daily prayers, nonviolent protests and sit-ins, all during the brutal, violent regime of the then-president, Charles Taylor. She functioned from a place of urgency—on behalf of people who had no voice and a nation being ravaged by war for absolutely no reason. She arrived at a moment of ferocious genius and shrewd desperation in the name of peace, and then turned the tide on a faltering peace process.

Dozens, then hundreds of women camped out around the hotel where warring factions were holding peace talks—which were going nowhere. The women sat on the ground and refused to leave. Instead, they passed messages inside to the lead negotiator and, at one point, even threatened to take off all their clothes to shame the negotiators. Their peaceful protests worked. Talks became more serious and within weeks, a peace treaty was signed. The civil war was officially over.

Peacemaking is a loud, messy activity. It does not behave and it does not wait to be convenient. It is audacious.

When I first met Leymah in London a couple of years ago, I blubbered in her presence. I realized in speaking with her how deeply encouraging observing her life and work has been for me, as a woman attempting to assert African female voices and faces into public spaces; in my case, the stage.

Growing up in southern Africa, I always felt a little out of place. I was a girl who was allowed to assert her opinions at home, to feel her voice mattered, and that her mind had things to work out, consider and share. But the world outside my house often told me otherwise, and the rules applied differently to me than to my male peers. That didn't feel "peaceful" at all. Inequality manifested, all around me, as oppression.

When I look at Leymah's work, I note she has never done any of it quietly. Peace is innately bold, and boldness has volume. To a loud-mouthed African woman like me, seeking to be part of change, this is affirming. Maybe, just maybe, my assertive girlhood self, who was hushed and threatened while growing up, has actually been on the right path. And little African girls coming up behind us, who may be feeling out of place, are reminded by our example that boldness and outspokenness is in our DNA by design: it is no mistake.

Invest in the next generation

I worry that many young people feel boldness and breakthrough are unattainable, that stepping out in the name of a better society, with your heart ablaze, makes you uncool or, as Leymah puts it, "undesirable." While chatting with Leymah in her New York City apartment recently, she spoke of young women—from prestigious places like Barnard College—who tell her they don't wish to be viewed as too smart, since that scares off the boys. But self-respect is an asset that she says girls must nurture in themselves to grow into peacemakers.

"The popular thing is, you have to be objectified as a sex symbol to make it," Leymah says. "This celebrity culture is really slipping into Africa. Let's look at ourselves. Say you are able to offer more to the world from here to here" (indicating torso from breasts to thighs), "then what do you put up here?" (pointing to her skull). "If you act dumb, he will continue to be dumb."

Leymah's people, the Pele, put this another way: "A child who washes his hands very well, eats with kings." For Leymah, "washing well" means hard work and respect for process. "In Africa, we have lost the culture of learning from older people," she says. "Everyone wants to be minister or president right after college. I tell them: when a child is born, she first lies on her belly, then learns to crawl, then takes her first steps. But all the while, adults are around, guiding her until she is ready to walk on her own."

Leymah's concern for the next generation reflects her own peacemaker spirit. Everything we do is so that children growing up behind us can experience a world better than the one we inherited. We do it one step at a time.

Peace takes perseverance

Leymah could have been just another victim; one more statistic.

But she dared to imagine a better tomorrow. She pursued higher education, gaining her a master's degree in conflict transformation and peacebuilding. Slowly but surely, she built a better life, not only for her own children—but for an entire nation. Leymah speaks now of how God used her struggles to make her an inspiring example to women struggling in similar circumstances around the world: "I am the Syrian refugee. I am the girl internally displaced in Lebanon and the woman at the domestic abuse shelter here in the U.S."

Leymah meets with a group of African feminists who get together every two years. At one point, they considered including men in their gatherings, but then decided not to do so. The space they have created is for sharing, being vulnerable, healing and rejuvenation. It is a safe place that gives these women the energy to return to the long and hard struggle. Leymah and her colleagues across the continent are unapologetically feminist in their approach to peace. It's a slow process, one that involves overturning social norms, some of which come from entrenched cultural beliefs and tradition. But women are raising their voices around the negotiating table and gaining respect.

Leymah told one story of how she had to intervene to protect a woman who was sexually assaulted by a very prominent man in Liberia. Other men tried to intimidate this woman and derail her testimony during the ensuing trial. Leymah stepped in, making it clear that she was well aware of the attempts to impede justice. She warned the men that she would expose their tactics to the media, and worse, if they persisted. They did stop, but not before trying to cut a back room deal with her to drop the case. Leymah refused. Peace means an end to business-as-usual.

Peace is hopeful

A mother, a wife, an author, a trailblazer, a rebel, a survivor of war and domestic abuse, a feminist, a Nobel peace prize winner, a peacemaker. Leymah personifies hope in all its transformative power.

What gives *me* hope is that there is a whole generation of African women leaders who are redefining what leadership is and what it looks like. Yes, there is much more to do, but we have already come so far. Leymah says not to have conversations over the coffee table and leave them there. We must go into battle and come out victorious. Women's issues are real and they are big, from female genital mutilation and child marriage, to sexual violence in conflict. But women are also out in front, using African solutions to solve African problems.

My time in New York with Leymah inspired and challenged me to do more. I also felt more than ever called to make sure the stories of peacemakers and *Sheroes* like Leymah are known far and wide. Little did I know as we began chat how much she would crystallize my life goals. But it makes sense to me now. *Super(s)heros* propel others to their calling through choosing to live courageously—and that what's Leymah did for me.

DANAI GURIRA is a U.S.-born actor and playwright raised in Zimbabwe. Her highly acclaimed Broadway play, *Eclipsed,* tells the story of five women and their tale of survival near the end of the Second Liberian Civil War. Gurira is well-known for her role on the popular television series *The Walking Dead.*

REBECCA MASIKA KATSUVA

Rebecca Masika Katsuva was a highly respected human rights leader in the Democratic Republic of Congo. After she and her daughters survived brutal sexual assaults in eastern Congo, she set up an organization that provides shelter, resources and compassionate care to survivors of sexual assault in conflict and their children. She died in 2016.

"MAMA MASIKA"

By Fiona Lloyd-Davies

Masika was a tiny woman, barely five feet tall, but she was a giant of a person. She was often in a hurry, and at the moment I am recollecting, she was irritated. I was holding her up. "Fiona," she says, "I don't have time to sit and talk to you. If I don't go out to the fields and get cassava, we'll all starve." "No problem," I say, "I'll come too."

It was 2011, and I'd come to eastern Democratic Republic of Congo to film her. I'd been slowly gathering footage over the past four years to make a feature-length documentary called *Seeds of Hope*. On each visit I filmed different aspects of Masika's life and work, hoping to capture her remarkable story. It's a tale of survival and hope lived in defiance of the nearly unbearable physical and psychological violence Masika experienced in her lifetime.

We are in South Kivu, a region of eastern Congo with the unrealised promise due to the abundance of natural riches and still trying to lose the long shadow cast by Joseph Conrad's novella, *Heart of Darkness*. Along with North Kivu, its infamous reputation only spread through years of war and violence, especially violent acts committed against women. A former U.N. special rapporteur on sexual violence in conflict, Margot Wallstrom, gave eastern Congo its toxic title as "rape capital of the world."

Here a civil war has waged, targeting women and their bodies, for more than 20 years. At the height of the war, it was estimated that 48 women were being raped every hour in the Democratic Republic of Congo. Such violence was deliberate: rape is surely one of the most effective weapons of war. The act fractures communities and tears families apart. Rape targets the very heart of society—the mother, the wife, the sister, the daughter. One woman knew this better than most. Masika was raped five separate times, all but once, by gangs of armed men.

***

Even in the driest season, eastern Congo is lush. Fields of golden maize, swaying in the breeze, grow shoulder high in weeks, their tassels seeming almost to touch the sky. Ferocious electric storms light up velvet nights, flashing pink and blue and quenching the thirsty land with plump raindrops. Nature is abundant but so, too, is violence. A true figure may never be established, but nearly six million people have died since the civil war began in 1996, according to estimates, while hundreds of thousands of people—women, children, men and even babies—have been raped.

Masika takes me off the main road and down a narrow, ochre-coloured earth path, under the sun's glare. The path is barely wide enough for one person, but an elderly couple still squeeze past us. The man holds a multicoloured umbrella over his wife to shield her from the heat. Masika has no such protector. Her own husband, Bosco, the love of her life, was butchered in front of her in 1998, at the height of the conflict. Uniformed men broke into their home, killed Bosco, and raped Masika and her two teenaged daughters. That event has shaped the rest of her life. Ostracized by her in-laws and thrown out of the family home, she left carrying just what she could fit into one plastic bag. Along with her two impregnated daughters, Masika was forced to find a new path.

Masika told me much later that it was the kindness of women that helped nurse her back to physical health and saved her sanity in the months immediately following the tragedy that ended her old life. Kindness also compelled her to follow their example. Her life since has been engaged with rescuing survivors of sexual violence, including children either orphaned or rejected because of rape. It hasn't been an easy job: the violence seemed relentless, never-ending and was often acutely dangerous. Soldiers raped Masika four more times to punish her for speaking out against them and their violent treatment of women.

She stops by a field of crops and picks some small chili peppers. Eating them raw, she tells me, "I never know when I may get my next meal." She's smiling as she says this, because hunger is not the worst hardship to bear. There are crops on all sides. It is harvest time and the bright colours worn by women workers stand out in patches against the green and yellow of cassava and corn. Some women are weeding. Others, with babies on their backs, are breaking off the maize and putting it in baskets. They chat to each other, sharing gossip and wisdom. Occasionally, you hear laughing. Pointing right, Masika shows me a section of uncultivated land recently given to her by an American donor. "In a few weeks," she says, "we'll prepare it for planting."

"This is my personal field," says Masika, pointing to another patch of ground. "This one with cassava trees growing up the side of a hill. It's the one I use to feed everyone at the centre." The warm greetings she gets from women working her field are telling. She is well-known here. Her work is valued by people who have needed her help in the past or may call on it in the future.

Masika was not an easy subject to film. All too often, I simply couldn't find her. These disappearances usually meant she'd received word of an attack on a village. There were probably women there who'd been raped, babies orphaned or even raped too. On many occasions, she'd walk days to a mountain village, find a woman survivor and carry her, on her back, to the centre or directly to hospital.

Her stories of rescue were astonishing. For example, she'd heard of a new attack in Ufamandu, a remote village in the upper plains that had been attacked before by the Interahamwe, the same militia from Rwanda who were responsible for the 1994 genocide. She and some companions entered the village to find dwellings still smouldering and dead bodies lying where they'd been felled. She thought she heard crying and started to hunt through the wreckage. Her companions said she was hearing the ghosts of the recently dead, crying out in confusion. But Masika was adamant: "I can hear a baby crying," she said. She kept looking and eventually found a tiny boy, still trying to suckle the breast of his dead mother.

She's showing me a pile of cassava roots, stacked and ready for her to take home, when her mobile rings. Everyone here is dependent on mobile phones, virtually the only modern invention that still works and keeps the country functioning—but only just. Masika is ashen-faced: it's bad news. A baby who recently arrived at the compound is now very ill. We must return at once.

We find eight-month-old Espoire limp, almost lifeless. Masika bathes him in cold water to reduce his temperature. One of the girls has a bag ready-packed. This happens all the time, I am told. "I found Espoire in a village after an attack," Masika says as we make our way to the hospital. "The village headman said that militiamen told mothers to throw their babies down and beat them to death. When Espoire's mother refused, they shot her dead." Masika found the baby with a broken arm and brought him here three months ago. "There are times," she says, "when I feel truly devastated. But then, when I find a baby without a mother in the middle of a pile of corpses, I can save that child. Who knows what the future will bring? I am devoted to these babies." She sighs. *"I must help them survive,"* she adds. *"They stabilise me."*

Filming Masika in the hospital, as she washed, dressed, fed or nursed young children, was profoundly touching. Many people called her "Mama Masika" because she has provided so many with the love, patience and nurturing that they'd either never experienced or thought they'd lost forever. She was able to give them something more valuable than medical therapy: constant, present love in an environment where fear, violence and insecurity prevail. She seems almost to collect the very young. At one point, in 2015, she had 84 children living at her centre. She dismissed the pleas of one non-governmental organization working with her to stop taking them in. When asked how she was going to provide for them all on so little funding, she retorted, "I can't leave them on the side of the road to die!"

It's rare in this life to meet a real hero, someone who risks all for the sake of others, but Masika was one of those people. A survivor of multiple assaults, she dedicated herself to helping thousands of others to survive their horrors.

When I first met Masika in 2009, I knew immediately that she was a remarkable person, someone who would leave an indelible mark on the world. She left her mark on me, too. I think of her every day, and remember her warmth, her smile and her immense capacity to love. Being close to her a few weeks at a time over a period of five years, I felt I was in the presence of immeasurable courage and resilience. She was, and continues to be, inspirational, and when my own life throws up challenges that seem insurmountable, I think of her. Masika reminds me that whatever happens, one tiny person can make a huge difference and bring new hope into another's ruined life.

Masika was a sister to me, and I was so honoured that she called me "sister" too. Having suffered so much in her life, death came for my sister quickly and suddenly. Masika went to hospital early one morning and died of a heart attack at 4:00 that afternoon. The heart that had given so much to so many finally gave out. Rebecca Masika Katsuva will not be forgotten, but she leaves a void that's impossible to fill.

"They think when they're raped that their lives are shattered. But we'd like them to know that it's not the end of the world."
Rebecca Masika Katsuva

FIONA LLOYD-DAVIES is a British award-winning documentary filmmaker and photojournalist whose work is focused on conflict zones and has aired on *BBC, Al Jazeera* and other networks. In 2013, she released *Seeds of Hope*, a documentary that details the life and work of Rebecca Masika Katsuva.

SHIRIN EBADI

Shirin Ebadi is an Iranian activist, human rights lawyer and former judge who won the Nobel Peace Price in 2003 for her work to improve human rights in Iran, especially those of women, children and political prisoners. She was the first Muslim woman to win the Nobel Peace Prize, and is a founder of the Defender of Human Rights Center in Iran and a co-founder of Nobel Women's Initiative. Her most recent book is *Until We Are Free: My Fight For Human Rights in Iran.*

DISSIDENT FOR JUSTICE AND EQUALITY

By Azadeh Moaveni

I met the Iranian human rights lawyer, Shirin Ebadi, one snowy winter day in 2000, in Tehran. I was a young reporter for *Time* magazine, accompanying her and a colleague to appear at an important trial. The previous summer, students at Tehran University had protested the closure of the newspaper *Salam*, an independent daily that was leading a fervently popular movement for greater press freedom. In reprisal, security forces and vigilantes attacked the students at their dormitory. They set fire to dorm rooms, grabbed women by their hair and pushed students out of windows. One student was paralysed by the fall; another, a poet, was shot dead. This targeted assault on students horrified the capital, and riots and demonstrations broke out across Tehran. It was the worst unrest experienced in Iran since the 1979 revolution, and the world, accustomed to a quiet Middle East, was transfixed. A cover of *The Economist* magazine at the time, showing a student demonstrator holding up a friend's bloodied shirt, captures the headiness of those days, when the anger of Iran's young people burst suddenly into the open.

On that winter day in 2000, Shirin represented the family of a student who had been killed. The courtroom was small and spare, and red-eyed students and relatives lined the benches. Shirin faced off against the judge. Why had police stood by so passively that night? Why hadn't they intervened to prevent paramilitary forces from attacking students? The judge was terse and the day's proceedings yielded little. No one was ever convicted for the dormitory killings, and authorities did not reprimand police. But I remember the electric atmosphere in the courtroom that day, and the expectant faces of the students' families as they watched Shirin raise her voice to demand justice and accountability.

Before the revolution, Shirin had represented the other side of the courtroom, presiding as a judge. Born to an educated Iranian family who believed in women's learning and engagement with public life, she had always wanted to practice law. Her mind was quick and alert, her temperament cool and fiery, and injustice simply offended her everywhere she found it. By the mid-1970s, Shirin had risen to office in Iran's highest court.

I didn't see Shirin again until she'd won the Nobel Peace Prize in 2003 for her long years spent defending the rights of women and children. As a reporter covering politics in Iran, I had followed her work closely. Shirin was at the centre of most anything progressive happening inside the country, whether it was pushing for equitable laws for women involved with divorce, inheritance or child custody, or representing the country's most famous political prisoners in court. She acted as legal advisor to the women's movement, which was drawing attention around the region for its savvy, grassroots strategies to engage ordinary women in legal reform.

In 2005, an editor at Random House brought us together to write *Iran Awakening*, the memoir of Shirin's life during the Iranian revolution and the Islamic Republic that followed. Day after day we met in the deserted breakfast room of a

Manhattan hotel as she told me her story: as one of Iran's first female judges she had supported the 1979 revolution, only to have the Islamists who came to power strip her of her position. It was the first time she'd had to sift through these memories in such detail, and as they slowly emerged from their locked away place, her face sometimes paled and her shoulders hunched.

She told me about her husband's teenaged nephew, arrested just after the revolution for possessing banned political pamphlets. It was only when the prison phoned his mother, asking her to collect his things, that the family learned he had been executed.

She talked about rebuilding her career in the early 1990s by offering legal advice to families, like that of a village girl who had been raped and murdered. Her family's struggle to ensure her killers were executed had been complicated by the Islamic Republic's twisted interpretation of sharia law. In the early 2000s, after a dissident couple were hacked to death in their own bedroom, part of a wave of killings by a state death squad, Shirin represented the couple's daughters. While sifting through police files, she came across the death squad's assassination list: her name was on it.

She recalled many such things, and cried, while I took notes, and cried. She was someone people sought out when their loved ones were in trouble, imprisoned or killed. She became a symbolic vessel for Iranians longing for justice, however out of reach it seemed.

We remain friends to this day, more than a decade after we first worked together. I often reflect on how fortunate I am to have caught Shirin in action in that courtroom years ago. I feel privileged to be the person she chose to relay her story to, for Shirin's life is the story of contemporary Iran. Her story not only illustrates how often women are at the forefront of movements for better governance and freedom, but also how their rights and prospects are the first to become caught in the endless pendulum swing between two perceived choices: secular dictatorship versus revolutionary Islam.

When Shirin and I spent time together in Iran in late 2005, the state had assigned "bodyguards" to protect her. She was receiving death threats under her front door at the time, and the guards accompanied us everywhere, even sitting at a nearby table when we were out to dinner. It was not entirely clear whether they were Shirin's guards or minders. As she said herself, what could you make of such people dispatched by a state that wants you dead? Authorities were nervous about her because she now had the global clout that comes with winning the Nobel Peace Prize. With this added layer of protection, she was becoming even bolder in defence of her clients. Shirin had already helped create a nation-wide discourse around women's and children's rights. Newspapers now carried whole sections dedicated to women's issues, from legal rights to domestic violence. Politicians who sought higher office began—for the very first time—to appeal to women's concerns in their electoral platforms. Shirin successfully advocated for progressive legislation around women's inheritance rights and raising the marriage age for girls. Before Shirin received her Nobel, the state found it easy work to crush a dissident's life without the world knowing. Now, when Shirin spread word of hunger strikes and deaths in custody, there were instant headlines around the world.

In the aftermath of Iran's contested presidential election in 2009, as Green Movement protesters were demanding the removal of Mahmoud Ahmadinejad from office, Shirin was outside the country. She stayed abroad in what became a kind of accidental exile, ostensibly until things settled down. But state authorities had made it abundantly clear, through ongoing harassment of Shirin's family back in Tehran, that it would be unsafe for her to return. We continued to spend time together, often meeting in London where my family lived and where she came often to visit one of her two daughters. It was a quieter period in her life, and we had more reflective conversations than before, when she had been a busy activist lawyer and I was a correspondent.

I noticed things about Shirin that I hadn't paid enough attention to before. She was the first woman I had met who openly considered herself to be both a practicing Muslim and a feminist. She didn't see much contradiction between the two. She said there was Islam, then there was patriarchy, and what a profound loss it would be to shun one's religion in the pursuit of gender equality, which did not need to be achieved at the expense of faith. She argued that it was an interpretation of Islam rooted in patriarchy that we must challenge, not Islam itself. Her stance is unique because Iran's intellectual classes tend to sneer at the least whiff of piety, while the books they write and opinions they hold are largely detached from the majority of Iranians, who are attached to their faith.

My own work is forever indebted to Shirin's views of gender and religion. When I look back at my writings from early days, I see the narrowness—a rigidly, secular viewpoint—and the ceiling it imposed on what I could understand in others. I know I have a broader scope today because of Shirin. Secular Middle Eastern feminists who say Islam needs a reformation might be more in vogue these days, and perhaps more palatable, but Shirin's politics and her world view have never centred on the convenient or easily digestible. She prays and quotes the Koran, but she also defends the rights of ethnic and religious minorities like the Baha'i and the Baluch.

Some critics like to say that Shirin's voice is less relevant now that she lives in exile, but they are usually the same critics who rush first to denounce her, who fear the words and ideas she continues to transmit from her perhaps not so irrelevant position abroad. The Iranian diaspora remains so mired in knee-jerk anti-Westernism, so determined to blame the West for Iran's isolation, that many of its leading proponents cannot tolerate hearing stories of Iranians who are victims of the current regime. It is an illiberal, flawed type of politics that we, the diaspora's children, carry with us. It is the type of politics that doesn't take personal responsibility for what has gone wrong with our country. I see this most sharply in reactions of my contemporaries to victims of the Islamic Republic. When a journalist is arrested they murmur that perhaps he was an American spy after all. When Shirin speaks publicly about the state arresting and torturing her husband, Iranian academics and intellectuals sitting safely in London or Washington often chide her: why air dirty laundry when such accounts only reinforce American pressure on Iran? By these subtle means, the diaspora absolves the Iranian government of bad behaviour because the West is the higher enemy and what we Iranians do to one another hardly seems to matter.

Often, when Shirin speaks publicly, an Iranian in the audience will stand up and rail against her for not blaming the West enough or for insufficiently defending some vulnerable minority group. She always nods respectfully, then redelivers the question: "I'm just one person. What have you done about this challenge you are expecting me to have fixed?"

Shirin once told me that she felt like she'd missed her daughters' childhoods because she was so busy working, sometimes locking herself in the bathroom to write. But while she feels she missed things, I see how much her daughters have been shaped by her work and the pride they take in her achievements. In the course of our long friendship, I have had two children and also struggle to balance the demands of work and motherhood. We were close enough that I confided in Shirin about everything— from cooking to coping with in-laws. I looked to her for guidance on how to manage a complicated life with dignity. After my children were born, it felt like I couldn't do anything well enough; my writing seemed less sharp, I travelled less for work and my in-laws seemed underwhelmed by my domestic performance.

I remember once feeling truly vexed about how to make quince jam go the proper shade of deep red. "Do I need a copper pot, is that my problem?" We were at a coffee shop in South Kensington, and Shirin looked alarmed and told me to go sit down. She brought me a coffee, sat opposite, and told me to listen carefully. "Azadeh, don't make jam. There are factories for that. And if your mother-in-law has no higher bar than jam-making, buy some jam, stick it in your own jar and offer it to her sweetly."

Like Shirin, I can't go back to Iran anymore. But being with her, knowing her, drinking tea with her, is the next best thing to going home.

AZADEH MOAVENI is an American-Iranian journalist and writer. A former Middle East correspondent for *Time* magazine, Azadeh is the author of *Lipstick Jihad* and *Honeymoon in Tehran*, and co-wrote *Iran Awakening* with Shirin Ebadi.

BERTA CÁCERES

Berta Cáceres was an Indigenous Lenca activist in Honduras who took on everyone from a corrupt police force to powerful landowners in her many efforts to protect the environment and fight for Indigenous rights. The co-founder of the Civil Council of Popular and Indigenous Organizations of Honduras, Cáceres was murdered in her home in March 2016, shortly after being threatened for her opposition to a hydroelectric project.

THE EARTH SPOKE TO HER

By Laura Zúñiga Cáceres

On March 2, 2016, they came into the home of my mother, Berta Cáceres. Hitmen entered the house of my mother, Berta Cáceres, and shot her in the chest. The heart of my mother, Berta Cáceres, stopped beating—and in that same instant, a grand ancestor and defender of life was born.

On March 5, rain fell for the first time this year. That was the day we planted my mother. The pain was enormous. I walked among thousands of people who summoned strength from the earth to cry out *Berta lives!* The heavens cried with us because despite the fact that she is now an ancestor who defends life and walks with those of us who struggle for life's continuity, the violence and hatred my mother had to suffer is very painful. It seeps down to the earth's soul. The world's pain concentrated in the sky as it started to sob with me. But the rain didn't get me wet, because my mother, Berta Cáceres, covered me and told me, in many ways, that she is still with me.

I hugged my mother for the last time in an airport the day before she was killed. She was sending me off. I was leaving Honduras because the threats against her had become constant, and my mother had decided earlier that my brother and I should live elsewhere to stay safe. She hugged me fiercely and told me that if anything happened to her, I should not be afraid. I wanted to believe nothing could happen to her, because my mother was the most invincible woman I had ever known. And now I've confirmed that, realized she transcended even death.

Many of life's oppressions weighed heavily on my mother from the moment she came into the world, in 1971. From the time when she could hardly walk, she was already witness to the violence of her father towards her mother. But despite carrying tremendous pain, Berta Cáceres would smile and write poetry for her brother, the one who left to go fight in and for another land. Berta, the child, punished for having been born female, rebelled every day against the limitations imposed on her. She stood by the women around her and defended them. Berta the child was full of love and art.

In school, my mother organized her peers. Berta, the young woman, built herself wings from dreams that she plucked from the air. She built collective dreams, hopeful dreams, together with the youth of her era. Berta often left Honduras to participate in social movements in El Salvador and Nicaragua. By the time she turned 18, Berta the young woman was living in poverty and was already being tracked and persecuted by government authorities for her activities. It was around this time that she gave birth to her first daughter.

In 1990, Berta gave birth to her second daughter. She was born premature. They surrounded her with bottles of warm water so she would survive, covering her in tablecloths. It was all they had to wrap her in. My mother filled her with love, an encompassing rebel love. Berta was now a schoolteacher in the Lenca communities, where there were no schools and where other teachers refused to go. She knew that to change the world we must use everything we have at hand, and her hands were enormous.

The great struggle to defend life led my mother to become the guardian of the rivers. In 1992, I lived inside of my mother. I lived inside the guardian of the rivers, the womb of a rebel. I heard the rivers running freely through my mother's body, I heard her heart, I heard her rebellion and indignation emerge from within her. I floated in her subterranean waters and when my time came, my great ancestor, the guardian of the rivers, the mother I inhabited, wove me a path that would lead me into the world. Holding me in her arms, she would organize the Lenca people. She would listen to their ancestral wisdom and would weave together with care and love an organization that she would struggle alongside of for the rest of her life.

The Civic Council of Popular and Indigenous Organizations of Honduras, COPINH, was born in 1993. This organization put Indigenous peoples, so long forgotten and made invisible by a racist society, on the national stage. The militant and rebellious COPINH led the way in the struggle to defend life, taught other ways to relate to one another, showed that the Earth is our mother. Mothers are to be loved, cared and respected—not sold. Together with COPINH, Berta confronted loggers, extractive industries that wanted to roll over people and build megaprojects, and those who attacked women. They demanded that governments respect peoples' rights and they accompanied the struggles of others with solidarity and love.

In 1995, Berta gave birth to her only male child, whom she nurtured while continuing to build COPINH. Together with my sisters and brother, we grew up in Lenca communities, where they gave us coffee while we listened in on the meetings where my mother stirred debate. She was a natural leader, able to include everyone's voice, deepen their analysis of local issues and help them express their views clearly. She never underestimated anyone, but encouraged people around her to overcome their fears. She was able to draw out the best qualities in everyone she worked with.

By 2009, my mother had become a national leader. In June of that year, when the army overthrew leftist president Manuel Zelaya, Berta publicly opposed the coup. We were together, sitting facing each other, alone. We listened to the radio attentively. It was a station from El Salvador, since no Honduran radio or television stations were operating. We looked at the ground while over the radio they read a list of the people who had supposedly been killed. They said my mother's name. I looked up and saw her looking back at me. I felt safe because I had her in front of me. Her name being on that list meant that Berta Cáceres was known, that she was an important figure for Honduran struggles and this put her at risk. Berta, the woman, Berta the Guardian, grabbed a backpack with the most basic necessities and headed to the capital to fight, to organize, to contribute whatever she could.

By 2016, my mother had been recognized internationally for her activism. She lived under constant threat. She waged one very special campaign: the defense of the Gualcarque River. Construction of the Agua Zarca hydroelectric project, comprised of cascading dams, was being planned and the Lenca community of Río Blanco, for whom the Gualcarque was sacred, opposed construction. The dams would not only obstruct their main sources of irrigation and drinking water, but also cut off supplies of food and medicine. Construction for the project was approved without consulting the Lenca, in violation of international treaties governing the rights of Indigenous peoples.

Berta put her body and soul into the struggle against that

project. For her, defending the Gualcarque symbolized the protection of all the rivers in the world. And respecting the Río Blanco community symbolized the recognition of all local decisions. The company behind the project, Desarrollos Energéticos S.A., supported by banks like the Netherlands Development Finance Company and the Finnish Fund for Industrial Cooperation Ltd., attempted to block their efforts. My mother was threatened, defamed and jailed for opposing the project. The campaign was successful in a number of ways, however. Sinohydro, a Chinese state-owned company, the world's largest dam developer and a partner in the project, pulled out of the project because of their campaign, as did a private sector arm of the World Bank.

My mother attended a final protest in defense of the Gualcarque on February 20, 2016 in Río Blanco, only two weeks before her death. Army, police and employees of the dam company confronted the protesters; some were threatened or detained. Attempts to intimidate my mother intensified.

On March 2, 2016, killers came into the home of my mother, Berta Cáceres, and shot her in the chest. The world felt the impact of the bullets, which went right through her breast. I imagine their trajectory, but I cannot understand how such small objects could cause so much damage to flesh, bone and love. The chest that was so immense to me, so warm and, since our final embrace, infinite. It hurts: the savagery, hatred and violence of the system that killed my mother. They strike us with misogyny and racism because they need us to be weak. They want the river imprisoned and their money to run free.

The reaction to my mother's death was international outrage, but the Honduran government still has not launched a proper investigation. Five people were arrested for her murder; two with links to the company heading up the dam project, two former military officers, and a serving army member. But the investigation into her death lacks transparency and authorities have refused to question high-ranking officials. The situation for activists in Honduras remains perilous.

In the very moment my mother's heart stopped beating, an ancestor was born. Her heart nests in the mountains and her blood veins the earth. Berta Cáceres, guardian of the rivers, opened the way to live for others. Those gunshots did not diminish her spirit, which still grows, keeps watch, and protects us. The strength, love, rebellion and hope of our grand ancestor accompany us always. My mother tells us that we shall prevail, that life shall prevail. We deserve the happiness of seeing our horizons become green again.

LAURA ZÚÑIGA CÁCERES is the daughter of Berta Cáceres. She is a youth activist who works with several organizations, including the Civic Council of Popular and Indigenous Organizations of Honduras, and *Hagamos Lo Imposible* (We Do the Impossible) in Argentina. She is currently completing her degree in obstetrics at the University of Buenos Aires.

SHANNEN KOOSTACHIN

Shannen Koostachin was a young activist from the Attawapiskat First Nation in northern Canada. At 12 years old, Shannen launched a social media letter writing campaign demanding a new school because the one in her community sat next to a toxic waste dump. The campaign gained national attention, and inspired thousands of children across Canada to write letters to the prime minister demanding proper schools in First Nations communities. Shannen died in a car accident at the age of 15, but her campaign continues through the Shannen's Dream Foundation.

I WILL NEVER GIVE UP

By Cindy Blackstock

First Nations Elders said Shannen Koostachin was a teacher, and that she had done her job. Those of us who knew her were not ready to let her go. She was just 15 years old.

Shannen was born in the Attawapiskat First Nation on July 12, 1994 under the stars of the Big Dipper—a constellation sacred to her Cree ancestors. The traditional territory of Shannen's people cuts a vast swath through Northern Ontario, extending along James Bay in a remote area of Canada. It is only in the last 50 years that Attawapiskat became a community with permanent buildings. For generations, it had been a seasonal camp for a people who lived off the land.

Attawapiskat's elementary school was closed in 2000, condemned because of a massive diesel leak that occurred several years earlier. Without a proper school, Shannen and the other children in the community went to school in makeshift portables. Conditions were dire in the portables. Despite outside temperatures of -40 degrees Celsius, there was black mould contamination, rodent infestations, and regular heat interruptions. Worse still, the school received less funding for teachers, books and other learning supplies than schools for non-Aboriginal children elsewhere in Canada.

Though young, Shannen recognized the injustice of having to go to school in toxic, broken down portable trailers.

In 2007, when she was 12 years old, Shannen and some of her friends launched a campaign on Facebook and YouTube— creating a video for non-Aboriginal children and asking them to write letters to the federal government in support of a new school for Attawapiskat. Children around Canada were shocked by what they learned, and they reacted. The federal government received thousands of letters from children demanding a new elementary school for Attawapiskat and other First Nations communities like it.

A year after Shannen launched her social media campaign, the government of Canada sent a letter to Attawapiskat First Nation saying it could not afford to build a new school in the community. Shannen and her friends had a meeting about the letter and decided to cancel their grade 8 graduation celebration. Instead, they used their graduation funds to send Shannen and two classmates, Chris Kataquapit and Solomon Rae, down to Ottawa to meet with Canada's Minister of Indian Affairs, Chuck Strahl.

Shannen later told us, "I think the minister was nervous." He preempted the discussion with the students, telling them there would be no new school for Attawapiskat. "I don't believe you and I will never give up," Shannen told Strahl. "School is a time for dreams and every kid deserves this." The Attawapiskat delegation was stunned. Shannen would not, and could not, normalize racial discrimination. Although her awareness of racism and discrimination had been growing, it was still so foreign to her that the minister could deny kids their basic rights.

I'm the same way: after a decade of fighting in court against the Canadian government, I still find it surreal that the federal government denies Aboriginal children basic rights in Canada.

At some point during her journey to build a new school, Shannen came to understand that the campaign was bigger than her school. More than 163,000 First Nations children across Canada were receiving less funding for education than non-Aboriginal children and many were going to schools in deplorable conditions. Chronic underfunding takes its toll, and is a real factor in the poor education outcomes of First Nations kids across Canada. Despite the setback with Minister Strahl, Shannen never gave up. She kept speaking with and inspiring people of all ages to take action so that First Nations children could get what she called "safe and comfy schools" and a proper education. She understood there was not a moment, or a childhood, to be wasted. People by the thousands, including me, were compelled to act.

By the end of 2008, Shannen was leading the largest child-led rights campaign in the country and she had been nominated for the International Children's Peace Prize organized by the KidsRights Foundation. As part of the nominating process, Shannen wrote a letter to me answering some of the questions in the peace prize application. I received her letter on July 28, 2008—Shannen had just turned 14 years old.

She wrote:

> *1. Of course, I would support others even though they are non-natives. I would help around and do whatever I can to support. This is why we made the circle. One is red, one is yellow, the other is white and the other is black. We are all the same. We keep the circle strong!*
>
> *2. So that he'll (Minister Strahl) know that we will not wait another eight years. He knows that we are sick and tired of walking back and forth outside in the cold winter,*

the cold wind, the cold rain, the hot sun. He knows that. It's just that he doesn't understand. If he did understand he could've just give(n) us a school just like that!

3. I would tell them (other children) not to be afraid. To ignore people who are putting you down. To get up and tell them what you want…what you need!

4. I would tell them to think about the future and follow their dreams. I would tell them NEVER give up hope. Get up; pick up your books, and GO TO SCHOOL. But not in portables.

She added a smiley face after that those last words. That was Shannen; she was very wise, and very much a loving child.

Shannen loved her culture and her community dearly, but later the same year she made the tough decision to leave Attawapiskat to go "South" to get a better education. Shannen knew that if she stayed in her own community school, the shortfalls in education funding meant she would not receive the education she needed to realize her dream of becoming a human rights lawyer. She made the heartbreaking choice to leave her family and community to go to school off reserve in New Liskeard, hundreds of kilometers away from her family in a town where her Cree language was not spoken. As she walked down the hallway of her new school she wandered into a classroom and began touching all of the books. Tears rolled down her face. When she was asked what was wrong, Shannen said, "I wish I had my life to live over again so I could go to a school as nice as this."

On May 31, 2010, Shannen joined family friend Rose Thornton for an end of the year trip to southern Ontario to celebrate her successful school year. Shannen had worked hard at school that year and was looking forward to returning to Attawapiskat for the summer to be with her much loved family and friends and to walk the lands of her ancestors. She told her older sister

Serena "I will see you soon." Those were among her last words. Shannen and Rose died in a car accident on their way home.

Within 24 hours of her passing, some of the thousands of children she had inspired created a Facebook page called Shannen's Dream to honour their friend and to pledge to continue her work to ensure proper schools for all First Nations students. In the months and years that followed, children gathered on Parliament Hill to read letters to the prime minister calling for an end to second-class health care, education and child welfare services for First Nations children. Shannen's father, Andrew Koostachin, credits the children for helping to convince the government to finally build a new school in Attawapiskat, and getting the House of Commons to pass a unanimous motion in support of Shannen's Dream. The children are not done. First Nations education continues to be substandard, and the children continue to write letters demanding better from the Canadian government.

On the day the Shannen's Dream motion passed in Parliament, I accompanied Andrew Koostachin, Shannen's mom Jenny Nakogee, and Shannen's older sister Serena on a visit with some of the children who had written letters supporting Shannen's Dream. Speaking to the children on behalf of his family, Andrew said, "Real leaders don't create followers, they create other leaders."

I've seen the magic of Shannen's spirit in many children who know her only through inspiration. A non-Aboriginal boy I know who always looked down from lack of confidence finally looked up when he was invited to escort dignitaries during the release of a Shannen's Dream report at his school. "Somebody needs me!" he said. Another boy tossed his Shannen's Dream letter away thinking no one would ever read it before gathering the courage to retrieve it and put it in the mail. That letter has inspired over 50,000 people in five countries. Daxton, a student who discovered he loved public speaking while reading his Shannen's Dream letter out loud to an audience, described Shannen's impact on him: "The best thing about Shannen's Dream is that you don't have to be a good athlete or be one of the kids who does good at school to make a difference. Everyone can help and everyone counts."

Shannen's leadership, both in life and in spirit, is a guiding light in my own work to achieve equity for First Nations children and families. Shannen's dream of "safe and comfy schools" was embedded in her belief that every child should be able to grow up and "be someone important." She did not accept racially discriminatory inequities in First Nations education funding, and she dared the rest of Canada not to accept it either.

Many Canadians are not aware of the inequities in First Nations children's services and actively judge First Nations children as if they get more than other children—when they are actually getting less. Internationally, many people find it hard to believe that a country like Canada would racially discriminate against children, so many people ignore the profound evidence that it is happening. Tragically, when the world around First Nations children codifies their hardships as personal deficits then the children themselves come to believe that somehow they deserve less.

Children know this treatment is not right. Shannen knew it, too.

There is hope that racial discrimination in public services may finally be coming to an end in Canada. In January of 2016, the Canadian Human Rights Tribunal made a landmark decision confirming that the Canadian government is racially discriminating against 163,000 First Nations children and their families by providing flawed and inequitable child welfare services. I filed the complaint on behalf of the First Nations Child and Family Caring Society of Canada in 2007, along with Assembly of First Nations National Chief Phil Fontaine.

The federal government tried numerous times to get the case dismissed on technical grounds, but was unsuccessful. It was a huge victory for First Nations children and the non-Aboriginal children who stood with them, but the struggle is far from over. Now we must push to ensure that the government respects this ruling and finally delivers equal services to First Nations children.

People often ask me what surprised me the most during the Canadian Human Rights Tribunal hearings. My answer is always the same: the fact that we had to take the federal government to court to get them to treat little kids equally. I am still shocked by that, and dismayed by federal arguments in court suggesting the Canadian government cannot *afford* to treat First Nations children fairly. As Shannen's life and work has demonstrated, there is simply no excuse for giving First Nations children fewer public services than other children. Canada is one of the wealthiest countries in the world but we will remain morally bankrupt until we fully address the profound inequities experienced by First Nations children.

The Elders are right. Shannen is an enduring and loving teacher who compels us to light our own candles of hope as we rise to be something better than we ever thought we could be, on behalf of everyone around us.

Shannen grew up under the Big Dipper. It is a sacred constellation, where each star symbolizes one of the sacred grandfather teachings that she lived her life by: love, respect, honesty, wisdom, humility, truth and bravery. When I miss her, I visit with the children she inspired and I see the light of her stars in each one of them.

CINDY BLACKSTOCK is a First Nations activist and the Executive Director of the First Nations Child and Family Caring Society of Canada. In 2007, she filed a complaint pursuant to the Canadian Human Rights Act claiming the Canadian government was racially discriminating against 163,000 First Nations children and their families by paying less for child welfare services on reserves. Finally, in 2016, the Canadian Human Rights Tribunal substantiated the discrimination claim and ordered the government to correct it.

TAWAKKOL KARMAN

In 2011, at the age of 32, Tawakkol Karman became the youngest person ever awarded the Nobel Peace Prize. In her native Yemen, Karman was at the forefront of the struggle for human rights and women's participation in peacebuilding for many years, organizing nonviolent protests that swelled in size and became part of the 2011 Arab Spring movements. She is a board member of Nobel Women's Initiative.

LEADING A REVOLUTION FROM THE STREET

By Hooria Mashhour

In 2011, when Tawakkol Karman won a Nobel Peace Prize for her work promoting peacebuilding and women's rights in Yemen, the world cheered her as the first Yemeni, first Arab woman, and at 32, the youngest person of either gender, to be so honoured. Those of us who had worked with Tawakkol in Yemen already knew her as a leader with power far beyond her years. To our pro-democracy movement, she was "the mother of the revolution."

Tawakkol grew up in the city of Taiz and the Yemeni capital Sana'a in an educated, middle class family. Her late father was a prominent politician known for his integrity and support of women's rights. "He was a forward thinker who said that his work represented the true Islam, which calls for liberation and rejection of injustice," she later said. "My father talked to my siblings and me as adults, and listened to our opinions, whose diversity made him happy. He urged his daughters to leave the traditional roles of women and participate in public life. My mother encouraged education, compassion, tolerance and altruism; he told me to be bold. When I was young, I jokingly told my father I would someday be Yemen's president. He said 'President only of Yemen? You have underestimated yourself.'"

Energetic, ambitious, and driven, she earned a graduate degree in political science, became a journalist, married Mohammed al-Nahmi—also a women's rights supporter—and was a mother of three by the time she was 25. "From the beginning, my husband and I agreed that our marriage should not put any obstacle in the way of my activism," she now says. "I always found time for it all. Maybe I got tired, but I was never bored."

Tawakkol's passion was grassroots activism. She began early, and became a singular political force. At a time when Yemen struggled under an autocratic, corrupt regime and many Yemenis were afraid to speak up, she broke the silence.

Under the rule of then-president Ali Abdullah Saleh, who came to power in the late 1970s, Yemen was a country known for gross human rights violations, press censorship, corruption, poverty, and want. International aid money and profits from natural resources like oil went to the wealthy and powerful while ordinary people suffered. Stunted, malnourished children died from preventable diseases. There were no basic health services, and young people, deprived of education, training, jobs, faced hopeless futures. Journalists who criticized the government risked arrest, even physical violence. Even members of opposition parties, who feared that Saleh would stop at nothing to remain in power, kept mostly quiet, seeking only minimal, limited reform.

In 2005, Tawakkol, who had become the first Yemeni journalist to do reporting via the Internet, founded the organization Women Journalists Without Chains. Its original focus was advocating for press freedom, but within two years the organization—and Tawakkol—was outspokenly demanding more. In a widely-circulated 2007 newspaper article, she argued that the government would never reform voluntarily. Yemen needed a popular uprising, one with a single clear objective, "the removal of the present regime" and its replacement with a democratic government. The means to make the change, she said, were peaceful sit-ins, demonstrations and civil disobedience. Tawakkol's own heroes, whose portraits hung in her office, were Martin Luther King, Mahatma Gandhi and Nelson Mandela. From the start, she emphasized that successful change came only through nonviolent struggle.

Publishing the article was an act of stunning bravery, not only because in it Tawakkol confronted power, but because she spoke up as a woman in a country where we had almost no visibility and few rights. As many as half of all Yemeni women were illiterate, 23 percent suffered female genital mutilation and one in five girls was married by 15. In 2008, Tawakkol took another radical step. She was a devout Muslim, who had always dressed in a face-covering black *niqab*. But in 2008, just as she was rising to speak at a conference that would be broadcast on national television, she removed her veil, and replaced it with a pale purple *hijab*. She later said that wearing the veil was a traditional, not Islamic custom, and "not suitable for a woman who wants to work in activism and the public domain. People need to see you."

In those days, I was deputy chair of the Women's National Committee, a small but outspoken government body affiliated with the cabinet and with the mandate of defending women's rights, and when I worked with Tawakkol, I was impressed by her tireless commitment. Women Journalists Without Chains monitored human rights violations, and opponents of Saleh used the organization to speak out against corruption. Tawakkol also became deeply involved in advocating for a group of villagers in the southern part of the country who had been evicted from their homes for not paying "protection" money to a tribal chief with ties to the Saleh regime. She organized and led scores of sit-ins and protests in Sana'a demanding that the displaced be allowed to return and that those responsible be punished. She even provided the villagers with tents, food, clothes and medication. Despite pushback from government officials, she managed to mobilize three parliamentary and judiciary committees to investigate their poor living conditions. She had an incredible ability to make things happen. Soon she brought together a coalition of journalists, civil society groups and political parties that organized "Tuesday Protests"—sit-ins in front of the president's cabinet office demanding regime change. I resigned my government position and joined them.

In 2010, President Saleh tried to alter the Yemeni constitution to allow for an endless presidential term, and people became increasingly outspoken in their rage. Huge waves of protest were passing through the Arab world, and soon brought down President Zine el Abidine Ben Ali in Tunisia, then Hosni Mubarak in Egypt. It seemed that anything was possible. Using Facebook posts, Tawakkol mobilized young people to attend protests, and in front of Sana'a University told cheering crowds that "Saleh's days are numbered! ..."

"Sisters!" she added, "Now is the time for women to stand up and be active without asking permission!"

For her audacity, Tawakkol was arrested and held in chains for three days. Public outrage exploded. The protest in what would be called Change Square grew until hundreds of thousands of Yemenis of all classes and backgrounds were in the streets—tribesmen, city dwellers, young people, even some army officers. And women! One journalist described seeing "thousands of women in black veils ... marching shoulder to shoulder." As soon as Tawakkol was released, she set up her own tent in Change Square and became the revolution's icon.

The risks were great. Tawakkol was arrested again, and government supporters attacked demonstrators with sticks and knives. Later, government snipers fired from rooftops, killing and wounding hundreds. Yet the demonstrations continued *peacefully*. To protect her family, Tawakkol sent her own children away, to be cared for by their grandparents. She later acknowledged being "very afraid for my children. But the Saleh regime was going to destroy anything, even hope. I realized that neither they nor any children would have a good future if it continued. Like other Yemenis, I had no choice but to follow the road of revolution."

Through the long months of protest, Tawakkol remained in the streets, brave, tireless, resilient. Her steady, clear vision helped her inspire disaffected youth who dreamed of a state founded on order and law, and she organized a youth council that remains an important force in the political landscape. Anyone walking through Change Square would have heard her voice over loudspeakers addressing the crowds. "Join us! A new Yemen awaits us!"

Tawakkol was in her blue tent in Change Square when word came of the Nobel. She later accepted the award as "an honour to me personally, to my country, Yemen, to the Arab women, to all women of the world, and to all people aspiring to freedom and dignity." The prize money, she said, would go to a fund for those wounded in the protests, and the survivors of those who died.

Within six months, President Saleh stepped down, and we began a national effort toward reconciliation and a peaceful transition to democracy. I became our nation's first Human Rights Minister, working to promote gender equality, abolish corruption, and end child marriage and female genital mutilation. Our new constitution decreed, among other things, that women would hold 30 percent of all elected offices. Tawakkol took an influential role as a member of the Reconciliation Committee, and also travelled to The Hague to ask the International Criminal Court to investigate the former president for war crimes. As a Nobel laureate, she became a global voice both for Yemen and for democracy.

I remember the hope we felt then, and when I think of Tawakkol's stirring speeches—"Together! Together we will create our new world!"—I wish they marked the triumphant end of my story. Instead, a few years after the Nobel ceremony, rebels backed by soldiers loyal to ex-president Saleh attacked and occupied Sana'a, overthrowing our democratically elected government. Fighting began between multiple factions and continues to this day, a catastrophe for the Yemeni people. More than 6,000 have been killed, nearly 1,000 of them children; there is almost no food and fuel, and a growing shortage of water. The advancement of women's rights has stalled. The situation is even worse than it was in 2011, when our people took to the streets.

Because of my work promoting women's and human rights, I received many death threats. In September 2014, after armed men arrived at my office, I fled the country, though I will never stop fighting for democracy and human dignity.

Rebel fighters attacked Tawakkol's home, and she, too, went into exile. But this woman who broke the silence in our country continues to speak out, against dictatorship, extremism and violence, both in Yemen and the world at large. She will forever be known one of the most outspoken advocates in Yemen's history. In a conservative country where women are afforded little public presence, it was a young woman who led us to revolution—and a peaceful revolution at that. I know she will work until a prosperous, peaceful Yemen prevails. As she once put it, working for peace does not only mean trying to stop war, "but also to stop oppression and injustice."

HOORIA MASHHOUR is a women's rights activist who became Yemen's first human rights minister after the country's 2011 revolution—a position she was forced to leave after the Houthi militia overthrew the government.

LATIFA IBN ZIATEN

Latifa Ibn Ziaten is a Moroccan-born French activist who lost her son to an extremist terror attack in 2012. After her son's death, Latifa dedicated her life to combatting radicalization through tolerance and interfaith understanding. She travels throughout France giving talks on the subject, and is the founder of the Imad Association for Youth and Peace, which aims to help youth in troubled communities. In 2016, she won an International Women of Courage Award.

A MOTHER'S FORGIVENESS

By Nahlah Ayed

Between speaking and taking questions, Latifa Ibn Ziaten had been on the school stage for more than three hours. Still at the front, she is now surrounded by children—mostly teenaged boys—and they are weeping openly. The boys embrace her the way younger children embrace their mothers; burying small wet faces in the crook of her neck, arms circling her waist. Somehow, despite their sobs, Ibn Ziaten holds it in.

Always, in her gaze, there is both motherly concern and a bottomless sorrow. But here, on this stage, her slightly pursed lips register bewilderment. She's sparked tears with her speeches before, but *these* weeping children have thrown her off balance. Yet when she occasionally breaks free to lift their chins and look directly into their eyes to comfort them, she is solid as a mountain.

You see it in her gaze, the way she scans you, seeming always alert for signs of distress. Ibn Ziaten is, above all else, a mother: selfless, generous and forgiving. That role has brought her to speak at this school—and it's what makes all her talks so transformative.

The fact that Ibn Ziaten is a seasoned mother of five is central to her story. The tragedy that only four of her children remain alive is crucial. Imad was a 30-year-old paratrooper in the French army—and his mother's confidante. On March 11, 2012, he was shot point-blank and killed by a troubled young man with a criminal past who claimed to have links with extremist groups. Mohammed Merah went on to kill six others: a rabbi and three children at a Jewish school, and two more unarmed Muslim French soldiers besides Imad, in a savage spree that shocked France and signalled awful things to come.

Imad was his first victim.

It is a story that Ibn Ziaten retells in every unscripted public speech. The story of how it happened. Of how much she screamed that day. There's also the story of visiting the scene of Imad's murder to search the ground for some hidden message from her child, but instead only finding traces of his blood. She speaks in the authoritative, gutted tones of the newly bereaved. And when she can no longer hold them in, the tears flow easily. But her voice does not waver. The lesson does not stop.

Ibn Ziaten goes on to relate how she subsequently learned the identity of her son's killer. Mohamed Merah, a wayward youth of 23, claimed in videos to be a member of Al-Qaeda. She tells of her decision to visit his neighbourhood and of asking a group of boys where he lived.

"Madame, haven't you heard? He's been martyred. He's a hero," the youths apparently told her.

"I looked at these youngsters; it's like they killed [Imad] a second time... I said, 'You see the mother that is in front of you? She's the mother of the first soldier that was killed by Mohamed." Ibn Ziaten's revelation turned their "hero" narrative on its head. The boys were apparently shocked and apologetic. You might understand if she hated them for their admiration of Merah or if she hated Merah's family. But she does not.

"He had no chance. He [was] a young delinquent, a youngster abandoned, a youngster who was not educated, who had no family love, he had nothing," she says. In that moment on the street, she recognized that Merah, and others like him, needed her. She of all people—a tormented grieving mother who had lost her son to intolerance—would become a tireless preacher for tolerance.

The first time I heard Ibn Ziaten speak was in Toulouse, where her son was murdered. It's a city she finds especially difficult to visit. But even here, she made the same promise. "I stand tall and extend my hand to the youngsters who are the cause of my suffering today. I have to help them. I have to extend my hand to everyone who asks for my help." Her self-imposed mission is to counter extremist messages and light the way for lost youths who may be French-born, but do not feel they belong.

Ibn Ziaten was born in Morocco and moved at age 17 to France, where she learned early to adapt to and embrace life in a strange land. In that way, her story is reminiscent of my own mother's. My mother arrived in Winnipeg, Manitoba from a Palestinian refugee camp in Jordan, via Germany, when she was barely 20. I've often thought what courage that must have taken. And what hard work it must have been to learn a new language, get used to a new way of life, start a job in a factory… what it must have been like the first time my mother saw snow. But while she was an outsider, like Ibn Ziaten, my mother worked quickly to adapt, and throughout her life she preached to us children the importance of acceptance and broad-mindedness. My mother is one of the proudest Canadians I know.

Both immigrants, my mother and Ibn Ziaten have now spent more time in their adopted countries than anywhere else. Like my mother, Ibn Ziaten was comfortable with her dual identity and proud of her place in her adopted society. She draws heavily on that experience when she speaks, and on ideas she's formed and tested along the way, to address difficult cross-cultural questions that are often raised in France and elsewhere. "Morocco is my mother and France is my father," she says, an elegant lullaby she taught her own children to help them navigate the difficulties of life in two cultures.

In some ways, generations of French citizens of North African origin *born* in France have had it harder than their parents. Those living in the disadvantaged *banlieues* or suburbs of France have it the hardest: with the lack of opportunities, ingrained racism, and the difficulty finding a sense of belonging all taking a toll. But Ibn Ziaten has told her own children—and thousands of others—that no disadvantage is an excuse to give up.

In her public appearances, she doesn't admonish or chide. In simple, patient language, she preaches a way toward belonging and loyalty to country without losing identity.

Early in 2015, I had the chance to watch Ibn Ziaten speak to several rooms crowded with children and adults. As always, she moved many to tears. Her soft voice carried across row upon row of schoolchildren seated in a cavernous gymnasium where I first began to understand her power. It was only weeks after the shooting death in Paris of ten people at the headquarters of *Charlie Hebdo*, a satirical magazine that occasionally features a caricature of the Muslim prophet. When the shooting happened, Ibn Ziaten was due to speak outside the country, but she changed her plans and remained, marching with thousands who took to the streets to show unity and support for freedom of speech.

At the time, there had been unrest and tension between Muslim and non-Muslim residents of Romans Sur Isère, a southern French town. At one school there, French children from various Muslim backgrounds had refused to observe a minute of silence for lives lost at *Charlie Hebdo*, believing it was hypocritical when the same respect isn't shown for Muslim victims of wars abroad. In that tense setting, I first watched Ibn Ziaten speak with children. She started her speech by explaining the concept of a minute of silence: it is a simple gesture of respect for the dead, she says. She then invites everyone to observe one for the French citizens who died, and everyone complies: including the children who had refused only weeks earlier. What was missing for them, she later said, was an explanation.

Ibn Ziaten spent another patient hour talking with teachers, providing them with advice, too. They had been amazed as they watched these same difficult children easily interact and weep with her—it was a connection they had never experienced. Later that same day, in an evening speech to adults from the community, Ibn Ziaten tells her story again. She then posed several pointed questions about the children crying by her side that day. They had affected her deeply. "What I saw really touched me," she said. "And I will leave with a heavy heart. I hope I will find an explanation for it. Because to see young people cry like that in a school—I don't understand. Is it me who touched them? Are these children missing something? Are they missing love? Are they traumatized by what happened? I don't know. But I have a lot of questions."

She spoke about *Charlie Hebdo* and her belief in the right of the magazine's staff to publish what they pleased, and her equal right not to buy the magazine. She spoke to the importance of parental guidance; to the hardships of growing up as a French citizen of North African origin, and to the reality of having to work harder—knocking on all the doors before giving up to people who kept them closed. Once again, she brought many in the room to tears. They stood to express their admiration for her courage and candour.

I admired her plain-speaking, her honest messages, her capacity for love and giving, despite all that has been taken from her. No amount of repetition seems to dull the pain of retelling, and nothing can assuage her feelings of loss. But she always hopes the children and adults who hear her story will take something away that might change their lives.

Just 40 days after Imad's death, Ibn Ziaten started an organization for youth and peacebuilding named after him. She works to steer children clear from all kinds of trouble, but especially from links with extremist groups. She's helped to save lives—like that of a young Belgian girl she persuaded not to travel to Syria to join an extremist movement. It was one small victory in what she acknowledges is a difficult, ongoing battle, in a war that the other side cannot be allowed to win.

"I am only a mother with a family and I fight this battle with dignity and respect," she says. When she laid Imad to rest, she made a vow. "I put my hand on his tombstone and I said, 'you are always there for me, you are not gone,'" she told me." I will fight until the end of my days to help these kids, so that you didn't die for nothing."

Her most potent weapon is forgiveness. She wields it for her son.

NAHLAH AYED is an award-winning foreign correspondent for the Canadian Broadcasting Corporation (CBC) based in London. She has reported extensively on Europe and the Middle East, covering several major conflicts and the Arab Spring protests. Born and raised in Canada, she is of Palestinian descent, and spent time as a child in a Palestinian refugee camp in Jordan. She is the author of *A Thousand Farewells: A Reporters' Journey from Refugee Camp to the Arab Spring*.

JUNE JORDAN

Prolific poet, activist and teacher, June Jordan was born to Jamaican immigrant parent in Harlem in 1936, and grew up in the Bedford-Stuyvesant area of Brooklyn. She was a passionate and influential voice for liberation, and was fiercely dedicated to civil rights, women's rights and sexual freedom. In her 1982 classic personal essay, "Report from the Bahamas," June Jordan broke new ground discussing both the possibilities and difficulties of self-identification on the basis of race, class, and gender identity. The essay became an important contribution to women's and gender studies, sociology, and anthropology. She died in 2002.

I AM TRYING TO FIND MY WAY HOME

By Aja Monet

I am reading June Jordan in January. It is snowing in Bethlehem and I am curled under the covers of a twin bed on the third floor of the Holy Family Hotel. I am sharing a room with a sister named Tara Thompson from St. Louis, Missouri. We are on a delegation in Palestine with Black movement leaders, scholars, community organizers, and artists. In this room, we bathe and rest to ready ourselves for the day ahead. We palm shea butter and smear it along our thighs and through the coils of our curls. Each morning, we hurry out of our room and wipe the sleep from our eyes. We are not here to rest. We witness the walls, checkpoints, displacement, and the militarized state surveillance. We weep with the stories of our comrades in Palestine and meditate on the similarities back in the United States. Our country is killing Black boys and girls, women and children, sanctioned state violence, and we are in occupied Palestine searching for an inkling of home. Is this solidarity?

I was born a Black woman
and now
I am become a Palestinian
Against the relentless laughter of evil
There is less and less living room.
And where are my loved ones?
It is time to make our way home.

June Jordan's words are some sort of conduit. I carry her poems through the streets of East Jerusalem, a book beside me, overlooking Hebron. What of the power of words? We live with the burden of making sense. Black women exist in the margins of language. And yet, June Jordan used language in a way that transcended words. She wrote with precision and walked us to the edges of language, reaching beyond borders. *And where are my loved ones?* I look around me, a delegation of comrades. The interior worlds of women are the only homes we've ever known. *Who are our loved ones?* A poem becomes the artery between us. June Jordan wrote of our solidarity, not only as it relates to our shared struggle, but also to our shared joy. The interior world is the last frontier of colonization. Poems rally us to reach for our beloved community. *Where do we feel free?*

In the Dheisheh Refugee camp, we all gather around to meet with representatives from Campus in Camps and it is as if we travelled to another dimension. Tara's voice wakes the room, she says, *This is freedom. This right here, for the first time in my life, I feel free.* It was a flash of a spirit, a presence; a feeling of being felt. It was an unspoken understanding. Tara is the patron saint of Black joy. She can shift the energy in a room just by her chuckle and grin. We crack jokes and tumble to the floor with hurt bellies. A gasp of air is a moment to sit still in our bodies. Some say, we laugh to keep from crying. We hold each other in our contradictions. It does not matter why we are smiling, it only matters that we live to smile again. No fear. *Is this freedom?*

These are our survival methods, love notes, smoke signals, and testimonials. Like June Jordan's words, it reminds us to attend to each other. Tara is forever my sister and also, to me, an embodiment of Jordan's spirit. It is the spirit of courageous solidarity. June Jordan warns us to diligently love and live or else we succumb to indifference. If we do not stand together against the horrendous crimes committed against humanity, on our shores and abroad, we become complicit in the suffering of others. This is how we have survived the unsurvivable. Women bear witness and strategize for liberation as we reach inward towards each other, a sisterhood. Home is not a destination. We rock back and forth between here and the horizon. Home is a drifting between here and there. Home is the calm between us that frightens a storm.

AJA MONET is an American poet, performer and activist of Cuban-Jamaican descent from Brooklyn, New York. In 2007, at age 19, she was the youngest poet to have ever become the Nuyorican Poets Café Grand Slam Champion. In 2014, she won the "One to Watch Award" from the YWCA of the City of New York. Her most recent book of poetry is *Inner-City Chants & Cyborg Cyphers.*

ACKNOWLEDGEMENTS

It took a global village and a great deal of love to produce *When We Are Bold: Women Who Turn Our Upsidedown World Right*. First and foremost, I would like to thank the book's 28 contributors. You have put aside your own book projects, along with much other work, to honour the women who inspired you, and I am grateful.

I would also like to thank the entire team of Nobel Women's Initiative and the Nobel peace laureates who work together under its banner: Jody Williams, Shirin Ebadi, Mairead Maguire, Leymah Gbowee, Rigoberta Menchú Tum and Tawakkol Karman. Without the support of each and every one of you, this book would not exist. I am particularly indebted to Liz Bernstein, who never fails to say "yes" to my ideas and whose friendship and leadership challenges me to do better in the world. Jody Williams gave me the gift of time to work on the book, encouraged from the sidelines and pitched in to proofread. Leymah Gbowee's wise words provided the inspiration for the book's title.

Funding for this book was made possible by the vision and generosity of Nobel Women's Initiative's circle of supporters, an extraordinary group of women who invest in other women. I especially want to thank Sarah Cavanaugh, who immediately "got" the whole concept, and Cynda Collins Arsenault, who quietly supported the project at a critical moment. I also want to thank Marci Shimoff for her wise counsel early on, and Nancy Word, Lauren Embrey, Melissa and Danny Giovale, Amanda Stuermer, Carolyn Buck Luce, Lynne Dobson, Elizabeth Fisher, Kaye Foster, Margot Pritzker, Marcia Wieder and Lynne Twist for consistently being gracious cheerleaders of our work.

An extremely dedicated team worked hard to make an idea into a reality. Ashley Armstrong has been my co-conspirator almost from the beginning, championing the concept, identifying potential contributors and doing extensive research on everything from publishing to promotion. She has been an invaluable sounding board, and her creative talent and passion for the project is visible in almost every detail of this book— from the title to the stunning photos. Thank you for lifting me up and for being so dedicated to telling stories that matter.

This book also benefited immeasurably from the tact and talent of Katherine Leyton, who helped to shape and edit many of the essays and offered real-time feedback and advice. Carol Mithers provided writing, research and editorial support, and played a significant role in shaping the essays about Tawakkol Karman and Nawal El Saadawi. Marjorie Leach lent her editorial and research talents to the essays about Natalya Estemirova and Elizabeth Becker. Jennie Strickland brought her eagle eye for errors and sense of humour to the project. Mark Fried kindly contributed his time to translate the work of contributors Lydia Cacho and Laura Zúñiga Cáceres.

On the production side, I am grateful to Silvia Alfaro for agreeing to take on the publishing of this book, and for bravely choosing to run a small, independent publishing house. A sisterhood circle that has included Rosella Chibambo, Susan Johnston, Rosemary Leach, Gauri Sreenivasan and my mother, Shelagh O'Rourke, provided invaluable editorial and design input. Jith Paul generously contributed his talents as photo editor.

Many people in the book world have generously offered advice and shared their knowledge. Lynn Franklin never failed to answer my emails and provide encouragement. Stuart Bernstein connected me to authors and provided invaluable suggestions. Our thanks for sharing expertise also go to Jaclyn Friedman and Shari Graydon.

The International Women's Media Foundation introduced us to journalists Bopha Phorn and Anna Nemtsova, and we thank them for their enthusiastic collaboration. Other important connections to authors were made possible through the friendship and efforts of Elizabeth Moreau, Kelly Fish, Lisa VeneKlasen, Silvio Carrillo, and Sheema Khan. Peace is Loud was also very supportive.

Kimberly Mackenzie came back from the motherhood trenches to help enthusiastically promote the book. Two women, both former volunteer activists at Nobel Women's Initiative, played pivotal roles at key moments. Sara Walde worked on the book in the early days, and Daniela Gunn-Doerge was with us in the final stages. Daniela took on administrative and editorial tasks, and also dove energetically into photo acquisition.

We would like to thank the following individuals and organizations for photo donations:

The Jane Goodall Institute
The Forgiveness Project
Cora Weiss
Louisa Lim
Elizabeth Becker
Niana Liu and Christine Ahn
Helen Caldicott
Casey Camp-Horinek
Claude Truong Ngoc
Marcela Lagarde
Minou Tavárez Mirabal
Haydn Wheeler
Fiona Lloyd-Davies
Mairead Maguire
Ivan Suvanjieff and PeaceJam

On a personal note, I would like to thank JP Melville, who

believes in this work, and Lina, Zayne and Mazen, who have patiently put up with a high level of maternal distraction, and sweetly asked me many times, "So how's that book going, Mom?"

Last but not least, thanks to you, our readers, for sharing the stories in these pages far and wide.

Rachel M. Vincent

PHOTO CREDITS

Berta Cáceres. Photo courtesy of Laura Zúñiga Cáceres

Betty Oyella Bigombe. Photo © REUTERS/James Akena

Charlotte Mannya Maxeke. Photo © London Stereoscopic Company/ Hulton

Cora Weiss. Photo courtesy of Cora Weiss

Ding Zilin. Photo © Louise Lim

Elizabeth Becker. Photo courtesy of Elizabeth Becker

Flora MacDonald. Material republished with the express permission of the *Ottawa Citizen*, a division of Postmedia Network Inc.

Ginn Fourie. Photo © The Forgiveness Project / Photo by Louisa Gubb

Gloria Steinem. Photo © Niana Liu

Helen Caldicott. Photo courtesy of Helen Caldicott

Jane Addams. Photo © Bain News Service / Library of Congress, USA

Jane Goodall. Photo © Stuart Clark / Jane Goodall Foundation

Jewell Faye McDonald. Photo courtesy of Casey Camp-Horinek

Jody Williams. Photo © D Legakis / Alamy Stock Photo

June Jordan. Photo © Louise Bernikow

Latifa Ibn Ziaten. Photo © Claude Truong Ngoc

Leymah Gbowee. Photo © Pete Muller

Mairead Maguire. Photo © REUTERS/Jim Bourg

Marcela Lagarde y de los Rios. Photo courtesy of Marcela Lagarde y de los Rios

Mirabal Sisters. Photos courtesy of Minou Tavárez Mirabal

Natalya Estemirova. Photo © RIA Novosti/AFP

Nawal El Saadawi. Photo © Haydn Wheeler

Rebecca Masika Katsuva. Photo courtesy of Fiona Lloyd-Davies

Rigoberta Menchú Tum. Photo courtesy of Ivan Suvanjieff / PeaceJam

Shannen Koostachin. Photo courtesy of Charles Dobie

Shirin Ebadi. Photo © Rachel Corner

Tawakkol Karman. Photo © AP Photo/Hani Mohammed

Wangari Maathai. Photo © Evelyn Hockstein

Printed in November 2016
by Gauvin Press,
Gatineau, Québec